MEXICO

Written by Peter McGregor Eadie
Peace and Quiet section
by Paul Sterry

© The Automobile Association 1996
First published 1991 as *Essential Mexico*
Revised second edition 1996
Reprinted June 1997
Reprinted as *Pocket Guide Mexico* 1999

Maps © The Automobile Association 1996

Published by AA Publishing, a trading name of Automobile Association Developments Limited, whose registered office is Norfolk House, Priestley Road, Basingstoke, Hampshire RG24 9NY.
Registered number 1878835.

Distributed in the United Kingdom by AA Publishing, Norfolk House, Priestley Road, Basingstoke, Hampshire RG24 9NY.

A CIP catalogue record for this book is available from the British Library.

ISBN 0 7495 2126 0

The contents of this publication are believed correct at the time of printing. Nevertheless, the publishers cannot be held responsible for any errors or omissions or for changes in the details given in this guide or for the consequences of any reliance on the information provided by the same. Assessments of attractions, hotels, restaurants and so forth are based upon the author's own experience and, therefore, descriptions given in this guide necessarily contain an element of subjective opinion which may not reflect the publisher's opinion or dictate a reader's own experience on another occasion.

Colour separation: Mullis Morgan Ltd, London

Printed by: Printer Trento srl, Italy

Front cover picture: *Cupilco Church of Guadalupe* (AA Photo Library – R Strange)

Contents

Country Distinguishing Signs

On maps, international distinguishing signs indicate the location of countries around Mexico. Thus:

(BH) = Belize   (ES) = El Salvador
(GCA) = Guatemala   (USA) = United States of America

This book employs a simple rating system to help choose which places to visit:

✓	'top ten'

♦♦♦   do not miss
♦♦   see if you can
♦   worth seeing if you have time

INTRODUCTION

Mexico has been a favourite holiday venue of
Americans for many years and is now becoming
a popular, long-haul destination for Europeans.
This special country offers a magnificent range
of scenery, and many fascinating places to visit.
The borders of Mexico have changed many
times in the course of her history. They could be
said to extend further south during
Mesoamerican times, when the Mayas were
rulers of all the foot of Central America, and the
untamed Indian tribes of the north lived beyond
the central plateau. After the Spanish conquered
Mexico and made it part of their empire, Mexico
extended considerably north of her present
border to include parts of California, Arizona
and Texas.

Today, Mexico is four times the size of Spain,
bordered in the north by the Rio Grande, which
threads its way from Brownsville to El Paso; but
no natural line of demarcation separates it from
California, Arizona and New Mexico, which are
now part of the USA. In the south, the border
runs along the northern edge of Guatemala and
Belice, cutting off the heel of the southern part of
Central America. The rest of the foot now
belongs to several other Central American
states. To the west lies the Pacific Ocean and the
Gulf of California, and the eastern border is
created by the Gulf of Mexico and the
Caribbean, giving Mexico thousands of miles of
coastline, varying from sandy beaches to
rugged cliffs. Mexico has hot desert in the north,
fertile plateaux, mainly around the centre, and
jungle lowlands. Two-thirds of the country are
encrusted with mountains, some of which are
always covered with snow. Altogether, 22 peaks
tower over 10,000 feet (3,048m) above sea
level. The highest lies close to Veracruz, where
Hernán Cortés, the Spanish Conquistador, first
landed. It is called the Pico de Orizaba and is
18,855 feet (5,747m) high. Two mountain ranges
stretch southward from Mexico's northern
border: the Sierra Madre Occidental and the
Sierra Madre Oriental, and they join like a string
of pearls south of Mexico City. Geological
pressures have also created several mountain
ranges around Oaxaca, which fall away at the

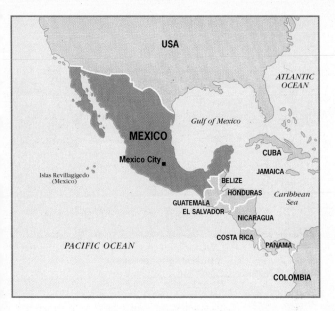

narrow isthmus of Tehuantepec on the southeast.

Volcanoes are plentiful in Mexico. The last major volcanic eruption took place some 45 years ago. A farmworker saw some smoke rising from a fissure and tried to smother it with soil, but was unable to do so because, after a small series of explosions, the ground opened up before him. Next day, enough ash had accumulated to create a 100-foot (30m) mound. Today this mound has grown into a volcano called Paricutín. It lies to the west of Mexico City and stands 3,000 feet (914m) high, with a crater which is 1,000 feet (309m) across.

Although there are many mountains in Mexico, rivers and lakes are few. The largest lake lies near Guadalajara, and is called Lake Chapala; two smaller but very attractive lakes are Pátzcuaro and Cuitzeo in Michoacán. It is worth touring these lakes by speedboat if you are in the vicinity. Río Balsas is the longest river; rising in the state of Tlaxcala and flowing into the Pacific Ocean, it is only navigable for short lengths.

INTRODUCTION

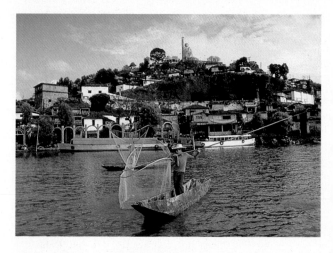

Bigger than the Statue of Liberty, the statue dedicated to José Morelos, a patriot of the War of Independence, dominates the island of Janítzio on Lake Pátzcuaro. On 1 November each year a commemorative fiesta takes place here

Something for everyone

Most people who visit Mexico follow one of three kinds of activity: visiting archaeological sites, of which there is an abundance, much on the same scale of magnitude as Egypt: visiting colonial towns, many of which abound with palaces, churches and cathedrals built during the days when Mexico was part of the great Spanish empire; and visiting magnificent beach resorts, bordering both the Pacific and the Caribbean.

When Hernán Cortés arrived in 1519 at the huge causeways of Tenochtitlán (the Mexico City of the Aztecs), there was no one to tell him that he had come upon one of the richest cultural countries in the New World; a country which could match any other in architectural magnificence, with over 11,000 archaeological sites.

Some 470 years later, much has changed, and visitors can take a classical tour to many sites and see for themselves. These tours usually begin in Mexico City, which was the former Aztec capital. Next stop is Oaxaca, to see the Zapotec and Mixtec sites of Monte Albán, Yagul and Mitla, and then on to Villahermosa to see the Olmec influences at La Venta Park, which started it all. The final stop is then Yucatán peninsula, which is studded with city states from the Mayan civilisation, whose inhabitants had a knowledge of mathematics and astronomy, far in advance of Europe at that time. An accurate calendar of 365 days had been worked out and their system of numbers was far superior to that of the Romans, which served our world for centuries. Site stops include Palenque, Uxmal and Chichén Itzá, all built on the grand scale. These classical tours provide the visitor with a startling insight into the great civilisations that developed in Mesoamerica prior to the arrival of the Europeans. To obtain the maximum benefit, it is advisable to visit the National Museum of Archaeology in Mexico City, which gives an excellent historical background to the development of these times.

Colonial Architecture

The period of New Spain lasted 300 years, from the victory of the Conquistadores in 1521 until Independence, and colonial architectural tours examine the influences and styles of this era. History offers no more rewarding field of exploration than the study of the interaction of two great civilisations.

When the Spanish conquered the Aztecs, Mesoamerican stonemasons could no longer practise their art in constructing temples and pyramids. Spanish architects, however, employed Indian talent in building early colonial churches. Hence much of the beauty of these graceful edifices is due to their skill and imagination. For instance, the intricate ceiling decorations of angels, strange animals, mysterious flowers and fruit found at Santa Maria Tonantzintla, close to Puebla, is a perfect example of Franciscan Tlamanalco, thickly adorned with charming figures.

Beach Resorts

As one would expect from a country that is edged with 6,212 miles (9,995km) of golden sand, Mexico has very sophisticated resort cities, including the famous Acapulco on the Pacific side and Cancún in the Caribbean. Developments are taking place continually, and among the new places to look out for is Huatulco, which, besides having several smart

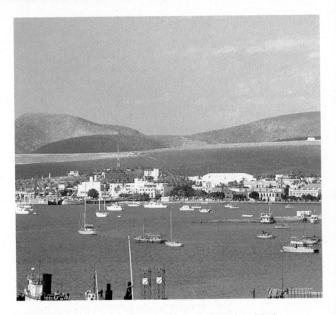

The resorts of Baja California are charming and the coastal waters surrounding this peninsula, which is longer than Italy, provide superb seafood. Social life is centred around small hotels who arrange fishing trips and scuba diving.
Swimming is excellent but beware of strong undertows

hotels, now has a splendid Club Med.
Off the West Coast and hanging like a pendant is the peninsula of Baja California, separated from the mainland by the Gulf of California. Along the shoreline here are resorts which offer some of the best fishing anywhere in the world. Ensenada is known as the 'Yellowtail Capital of the World' and the locals claim in Cabo San Lucas and San José del Cabo that 40,000 marlin are caught every year in water off the capes.
From the coastal towns of Los Mochis, on the mainland side of the Gulf of California, to Chihuahua runs one of the world's most scenic railway routes. It takes 12 hours and passes through the Copper Canyon, which is larger and higher than the Grand Canyon in the USA.
The exceptional coastline has more than enough room to accommodate a variety of holiday resorts, ranging from quiet venues that were once fishing villages to Cancún, which attracts over a million visitors a year with its high life and sizzling entertainment.

BACKGROUND

Origins

The earliest trace of *homo sapiens* found in
Mexico was uncovered some 25 years ago
during road construction developments near
the archaeological site of Tipacoya. Radio-
carbon dating indicates that these remains are
20,000 years old.

In most parts of the continent to the north of
Mesoamerica the early economy was based on
hunting and gathering. Only at a comparatively
later date than in Mesoamerica did agricultural
development take place in certain regions of
North America, whereas in Mexico explorations
over a wide area, stretching from Chiapas to
Tamanlipas, have established that early species
of wild maize corn were intensively gathered
and eventually cultivated. Research shows that
the evolution of wild corn to full cultivation took
place between 8,000BC and 1,000BC. Such
agricultural development would have been
essential to the creation of the early city states
of Mesoamerica.

Before the Spaniards arrived, and when there
were no cities in North America, it is estimated
that there were up to 20 million Indians living in
city states in Mexico. These figures reflect the
high level of civilisation which existed in
Mesoamerica in Pre-Columbian times. The
Europeans decimated these numbers by
bringing with them diseases against which the
Indians had no resistance, and by cruelly
overworking the Indians in near starvation
conditions. By the 17th century the pure-
blooded Indians who provided the main labour
force had dwindled from some nine million on
the Mexican central plateau to two and a half
million.

Following the conquest, Mexico's population
was divided into a caste system as well defined
as that found among the Hindus. At the top of
the pile were the *gachupines*, who were
Spaniards born in Spain. They had control of
both spiritual and political life and all
government officials belonged to this group.
Next came the Creoles who, although born in
Mexico, were pure-blooded Spaniards. They
were denied government office but many were

wealthy, thanks to the exploitation of cheap labour from the Indians who worked their *encomiendas* or mines. The third category were the *mestizos*, who were of mixed Spanish and Indian blood. Unlike the English and Dutch settlers who came to live on the eastern seaboard of North America, the Spaniards brought very few European women with them; hence, unions were formed with Indian women. One of the astonishing facts about New Spain is the small number of Europeans who came to live in Mexico during the first three centuries following the conquest. A census taken in 1793 showed that only 8,000 Europeans were spread throughout the whole country. The fourth category are the Indians, at the bottom of the social pile, many of whom are still suffering from a legacy of exploitation.

The population of Mexico today is 85 million, with 23 million living in Mexico City. The government is trying to spread the population more evenly through employment schemes, but still 2,000 people move to Mexico City each day in search of work.

Olmecs

The Olmec civilisation is popularly considered the mother culture, and her heartland spread over 11,350 square miles (29,396 sq km) on the shores of the Caribbean, now mainly the jungles of southern Veracruz and Tabasco. Today, the antiquities of the Olmec civilisation are more likely to be found in museums than on original sites. The Olmecs venerated the Jaguar as supernatural and many of their artefacts found throughout Mexico feature human beings with the snub nose of a cat and fangs.

Three main archaeological sites have been discovered within the Olmec heartland: San Lorenzo, with its remarkably advanced system of drainage; La Venta, where there is now a park in which the visitor can see several colossal heads which are 10 feet (3m) high and weigh up to 20 tons/tonnes. Stone sculpture is the supreme hallmark of Olmec art and in the park can also be seen caparisoned figure reliefs, stelae and rock carvings; and Tres Zapotes, which came into being after La Venta, around 500BC, and went on until 100BC, and which stretches along the bank of the Hueypan River.

Teotihuacános

After a long process of development, the Mesoamerican inhabitants of the Valley of Mexico founded the city of Teotihuacán, some 30 miles (48km) northeast of the present capital. Greater than contemporary Imperial Rome, the city was probably the finest ever built in Mexico. It covered an area of 14 square miles (36.26 sq km) and at its height had a

At the head of the sacred avenue of Teotihuacán, which runs like a spine down the ceremonial centre, is the Moon Pyramid, seen here. At the heart is the gigantic Sun Pyramid and at the foot is the Quetzalcoatl Pyramid. Together they represent the Trinity of the Teotihuacános

population of over 200,000 people. Development in Teotihuacán (the name means 'the place where men become gods') spans a period of nearly 900 years, beginning around 100BC and ending around AD750. The grandeur of the site is seen to lie along a broad thoroughfare known as the 'Avenue of the Dead'. Along this most sacred artery is a series of stone platforms known as *talud-tableros*. When the city was inhabited these formed a stone frame for magnificent murals, and were a constant reminder that this was a city of the gods. At the heart of the city is the giant Pyramid of the Sun, rising to a height of 200 feet (61m).

At the other end, the *Ciudadela* is dominated by a splendid six-tiered temple dedicated to Quetzalcoatl – the serpent god, and Tlaloc – the rain god. Both are of supreme importance in Mexican mythology. During its long history, Teotihuacán extended its influence through the valleys of Mexico, Puebla, Tlaxcala and Morelos, and stretched as far as Chametla near the coastal town of Mazatlán, some 900 miles (1,440km) distant. Penetration along the Gulf was equally strong, reaching from Cerro de las Messos in the south to Huexteca in the north. Traces of her culture have also been found in the northwest.

Toltecs

When the Teotihuacános finally abandoned their city, new groups from the north descended on to the Central Plateau. As time passed, these tribes converged and became known as the Toltecs. Their capital became Tula, an archaeological site 50 miles (80km) north of Mexico City in the state of Hidalgo. This is considered to be the legendary Tollan from which the Toltec culture dominated Mesoamerica from AD859 to 1250. After the demise of Teotihuacán, other cities such as Xochicalco, Cholula and Cacaxtla grew in importance.

Of primary interest in Tula is the Temple of Tlahuizcalpantecuhtli, dedicated to the morning star – Quetzalcoatl – in one of his manifestations. On the platform stand giant warrior sculptures 16 feet (4.8m) high. They look out over the landscape as though remembering back a thousand years to their once great civilisation. They originally supported the wooden roof of the temple, which has long since disappeared. On the chest of each warrior is a stylised butterfly, the Toltec emblem.

In the mythology of the Mesoamerican civilisations of the Central Plateau, Quetzalcoatl was the bearded god of learning and priesthood and during the Toltec period there arose a great priest, whose name was Ce Acatl Topilzin, and who founded the city of Tula. Because of his deep wisdom he began to be called Quetzalcoatl, and for the first time this name became linked with a man of ideas and spiritual development. His reign is remembered as one of peace and plenty. Legend told that he would return in the future and when Hernán Cortés landed in Mexico the Aztecs thought at first that he was Quetzalcoatl returning, which created terror in the hearts of their leaders.

The ceremonial centre of this ancient city contains a ball-court and the remains of other

Sixteen-foot stone warriors, atlantes, once supported the roof of this Temple of the Morning Star in Tula. On the chest of each warrior is a stylised butterfly, the Toltec emblem. Their sandals are decorated with serpents, a reminder that the pyramid is dedicated to the great serpent god Quetzalcoatl in his role as the Morning Star

interesting constructions, including flagstone avenues, colonnades, and *talud-tableros*.

Totonacs

The Totonac civilisation reached its peak between AD700 and 1100, and El Tajín is its most famous city. Set in the densely-forested regions in the state of Veracruz, these splendid ruins include the impressive Pyramid of Niches, whose 365 niches represent the days of the year.

An important ceremony, to which the Totonacs subscribed, was the dance of El Volador, which was performed as a religious rite. It is most impressive and can still be seen as a folklore spectacle, particularly in nearby Papantla. It used to take place only on the feast of Corpus Christi, but can nowadays be seen on most Sundays in the main square. Five performers climb to the top of a very high pole, which has four extended arms like a cross at the top. One performer stands at the top on a small platform in the centre, where he dances and plays haunting music on his pipe, and occasionally beats a small drum attached to his waistband, while the others, dressed to represent the colourful plumage of the macaw, the symbol of the sun, secure themselves by the ankle with ropes and leap off into space, with arms extended. All four encirclements of 13 makes up the mystical figure of 52, to represent the 52-year cycle of ancient Mesoamerica.

The Zapotecs and Mixtecs

The ruins of the sacred city of the Zapotecs lies just outside the beautiful colonial town of Oaxaca. It is called Monte Albán, meaning 'White Mountain'. To build this city the Zapotecs had to level the summit, construct retaining walls and lay out terraces. On top of the mountain are long rows of tombs in parallel lines flanking the plaza. Many elaborate tombs have been found stocked with funerary urns, which portray their different gods. They were also filled with precious stones and the walls were painted with frescos.

The first traces of civilisation in the Monte Albán area are thought to go back 1,000 years before Christ. It is interesting to note that although the Zapotecs lived in this region for centuries, the height of their civilisation corresponds with the

The sacred site of Monte Albán seems suspended between earth and sky like a magic carpet. On the levelled Gran Plaza stands the Observatory (front) and 20 other sacred buildings. The whole is set like a jewel in a circle of mountains 10,000 feet (3,077m) above sea level

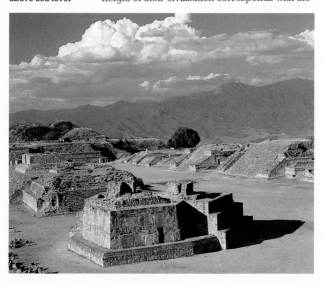

classical age of Teotihuacán. Cultural influences were received from outside their domain, but because of their geographical isolation the Zapotecs naturally developed their own distinctive style of architecture.

By about AD900, the Zapotecs began departing from the city and rival Zapotec cities in the Oaxaca Valley began to assume authority. The ruins of the two most important of these, Yagul and Mitla, are easily reached by car in a couple of hours' drive from Oaxaca.

The Mixtecs came through the Coixtláhuaca Pass into the Oaxaca Valley some time after the Zapotecs. They took over Monte Albán and revitalised it in their own style. The Mixtecs' claim to fame lay in their fine craftsmanship in precious metals, and their skill in the field of ceramics, with their potteries producing delicate vessels decorated with geometric motifs, glyphs and images of their gods. They also excelled in the production of turquoise mosaics. Mixtec history is well recorded in codices made from strips of deer skin joined together, often to a length of 25 feet (10.6m). On them were beautiful explanatory paintings of important events. These skins were usually folded like screens and stored as books.

When the new tribe of Aztecs entered Mexico from the north and overran central Mexico, the Mixtecs frequently found themselves conquered in battle and having to pay tributes to Tenochtitlán. Both the Zapotecs and the Mixtecs survived these hardships and those put upon them by the Spaniards, and today their descendants can be seen dressed in striking Indian attire going about their daily lives in Oaxaca.

The Maya

The Maya were the largest homogenous group of Indians north of Peru, and their cultural development began around 1500BC. The geographical scope of their civilisation is divided into three major regions.

The southern region comprises the Guatemalan Highlands, part of Chiapas, Pacific coastal Guatemala and a section of El Salvador. The central region, sometimes referred to as the southern lowlands, includes the Peten of

Guatemala, the Usumacinata River drainage into Tabasco, Belice, the Montagua River of Guatemala, southern Campeche and westernmost Honduras. The northern region contains the rest of the Yucatán peninsula, with many magnificent sites.

Many Maya cities, still in an interesting state of preservation, are designed along similar lines as other Mesoamerican cities. At the centre of the city were the main temples and spacious plaza. These were the places where important religious and anniversary rituals were celebrated. Close to this area were the homes of the priests and the lords and officials who were responsible for government and administration. Further out were the houses of the rich and important merchants, and on the perimeter were the dwellings of ordinary citizens, including the farmers who worked the land surrounding the city and supplied the food for the populace.

Ancient Maya achievements in art, writing, architecture, astronomy, mathematics and medicine rivalled those in ancient Egypt and classical Greece. Their mathematicians invented the concept of 'zero' and the value of position with numbers, when Europeans were struggling with Roman numerals. Thus the Maya were able precisely to measure time and astronomical events such as eclipses over millions of years. They also understood many planetary cycles and carried out complicated surgery without pain through their knowledge of herbal drugs.

The religion and myths of the Maya, and for that matter most of the Mesoamerican cultures prior to the Aztecs, was highly developed. The divine man Kukulkan (Maya) or Quetzalcoatl (Toltec) is depicted in legend as a Christ-like figure with a 'virgin birth' who at death was resurrected to a higher level in the universe. He promised a second coming. Pictorially, he is also represented as the sacred feathered serpent throughout Mesoamerican sites. Today we know too little about this religion because early missionaries burnt the original texts, but sufficient to realise that had the Europeans come to learn, instead of to teach and plunder, there would have been a cultural renaissance

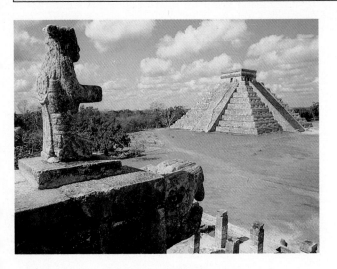

The Pyramid of Kukulkan at Chichén Itzá is a calendar in stone. Up the centre of each of the four sides are 91 steps. These add up to 364 and the final step into the temple makes 365, one for each day of the year. This complex pyramid embodies a host of astronomical information

instead of a travesty resulting in spiritual genocide of the Indian people.

Since the coming of Europeans to the New World, the Maya people have been subjected to break up and theft of their lands, and a varying degree of treatment than runs contrary to all human rights. Recently, however, Mexico, Belize, Guatemala, Honduras and El Salvador have launched a 'Mundo Maya' project to protect the lands of the Maya people, to develop ecotourism, and to raise the standard of living of the indigenous people. For this is a land of very poor people where conservational aims must rank second to survival.

The success of this project is essential to the well being of Mexico as well as other nations in Central America. The signing of the Copan Declaration in 1993 by all five heads of government listed above 'promising to work together for the defence, conservation, research and diffusion of the archaeological, historical and natural heritage of the Mundo Maya' should be a big step forward to a better future.

The Aztecs

In the chronology of Mesoamerican Indian civilisations, the Aztecs arrived late. They came down from Aztlán (Place of Herons) in the Mexican Highlands in the early 13th century. During their migration they acquired the name Mexica.

After wandering the marshes in the region of the Mexico Valley, they came across an eagle perched on a cactus devouring a snake. This fulfilled an ancient tribal prophesy, and here they knew they must settle and build their home. This they did and Tenochtitlán became the home of the Aztec or Mexican people. The eagle devouring the serpent remains to this day the heraldic symbol at the centre of the Mexican flag.

The capital grew into one of the greatest cities the world has ever seen, according to the Spanish conquistadores. It housed a population of a quarter of a million people and was laid out with a great criss-cross of canals. A model of it can be seen in the Museo Nacional de Antropolígía (Museum of Anthropology) in Mexico City.

Magnificent causeways, capable of carrying 20 soldiers abreast, linked the capital on Lake Texcoco to the mainland on three sides. The centre of the city, close to where the main cathedral stands today, was a giant pyramid, with its twin temples dedicated to Tlaloc the rain god and Huitzilpochtli the sun god. Surrounding this great capital, were farmlands that provided the produce which fed the city populace and enabled Tenochtitlán to become the ecclesiastical, civil and military centre of a great empire. In their effort to eradicate all other religious beliefs, the Spaniards unfortunately did a very thorough job of destroying and dismantling Tenochtitlán, even to the point of filling in the canals and much of the lake upon which it was built.

Although little remains of Tenochtitlán, there are some minor remains of Tenayuca in the suburbs of Mexico City, and some smaller Aztec pyramids at Santa Cecilia and Calixtlahuaca. Well worthwhile is a visit to Malinalco, dramatically set in the mountains some 30 miles (48km) from Toluca. Here you will see a temple dedicated to two great military orders of the Aztecs, the Knights of the Jaguar and the Knights of the Eagle. Aztec sculpture has fared better than architecture, and two particularly fine monumental works excavated in the 18th century can now be seen in Hall 7 in the Museo Nacional de Antropoligía. Great as the Aztec civilisation was, its role in the history of the New World was similar to that of Ancient Rome to Greece. Although it continued to improve building and engineering skills, it also marked the onset of decadence and a move away from original religious thought.

The Spanish Conquest

In the latter part of the 15th century Christopher Columbus, on an expedition funded by the Spanish Crown, discovered the island of Cuba, which lies off the east coast of Mexico. Cuba became the base from which Hernán Cortés set sail for Mesoamerica in 1519.

Cortés landed in Veracruz, whence legend said Quetzalcoatl sailed a few centuries earlier, promising to return. Cortés, who also had a fair skin and beard, actually arrived in the year prophesied for the god's return. The scouts of Moctezuma, leader of the Aztecs, reported that

The Conquistador, Hernán Cortés, wrote to the king of Spain to say that the waterborne Aztec capital Tenochtitlán was the most beautiful city he had ever seen. The Spaniards then dismantled Tenochtitlán and drained the lakes in order to build Mexico City

BACKGROUND

Cortés had embarked from a 'floating mountain', which also heightened the atmosphere of fear and awe. The arrival of horses which were unknown to the Indians and thought to be four-legged creatures with men issuing from their backs, and the Spaniards' ability to kill from afar using muskets, strengthened the belief that Cortés was a god. These are some of the ingredients which led, against unbelievable odds, to a few Spanish adventurers conquering a vast empire. Within two years of landing, Cortés was to bring about the surrender of the Aztecs. Before leaving for his trek through the interior to the capital of Mexico, Cortés ordered the ships in which his party arrived to be burnt, so that there could be no retreat. This act did much to concentrate the minds of his soldiers to the task in hand, for it was now a case of conquer or die.

Cortés was extremely skilful at winning over people to his cause, thus increasing the size of his army. In this, he was considerably helped by the behaviour of the Aztecs, who were continually demanding heavy tributes and men for sacrifice from outlying tribes. Considerable resentment against the centralised rule of

On Good Friday 1519 the Spaniards pitched camp on the Mexican coast and because it was Easter christened the place 'La Villa de la Vera Cruz'. From here the Conquistador marched his soldiers and newly found Indian allies through the bitterly cold high sierras to the Aztec capital of Tenochtitlán

Tenochtitlán had already built up. Those tribes who were opposed to the conquistador's ambitions were savagely massacred.

When Cortés had completed his long march, climbing the high pass between the mountains of Popocatépetl and Iztaccíhuatl, Moctezuma came out along the southern causeway to welcome him. The Spaniards were treated with great hospitality. They were housed as honoured guests in the palace of Axayacatl, the former home of Moctezuma's father.

Now, in a daring stroke, Cortés took Moctezuma captive and changed a potentially dangerous situation in which he could have been ambushed to one of being in control.

Cortés had to return to Veracruz and during his absence some of his Spanish troops in Tenochtitlán slaughtered many Aztec nobles while they were performing a ritual dance to their gods.

The Aztecs, incensed at this affront, waited until Cortés returned before launching a savage attack. Cortés was severely routed, but he rounded up huge numbers of new Indian recruits and returned to the fray. In the battle which ensued the defenders of Tenochtitlán stood little chance. After a courageous defence, under the new Aztec leader, Cuauhtémoc, the capital fell to the Spaniards. The demise of the great Indian nation had begun.

It is interesting to note nowadays where Mexican sympathies lie in all this bloodbath of wars. Today there are no statues to Cortés, and the revival of interest in those times is mainly due to attempts to re-understand the great Mesoamerica Indian civilisations that existed prior to the founding of New Spain.

Colonial Mexico

Following the construction of the capital of New Spain on the ruins of the old Aztec capital, the country was now divided into huge estates or *encomiendas* under some 500 Spanish landlords. In return for 'looking after' the conquered Indians by educating them in European ways and converting them to the Catholic faith, the estate owners were entitled to their unpaid labour. This privilege was soon exploited and could be said to be a strong contributing factor to the later overthrow of colonialism.

In 1535, Antonio de Mendoza was appointed the first of 61 viceroys who were to rule Mexico for the next three centuries. He was a practical man, whose portrait can be seen in the Gallery of Viceroys in Chapultepec Castle. His rule, and that of Cortés, saw the expansion of New Spain as far south as Honduras, as far north as Kansas and as far east as New Orleans.

As a result of their expansion, the Spanish were able to mine the mineral resources, particularly of silver and gold, of this enormously rich territory. With this wealth they built many beautiful cities with magnificent cathedrals and fine mansions. When the Aztecs were conquered, the Mesoamerican stonemasons could no longer practise their art in the building of pyramids and temples. However, Spanish architects soon employed their talents in the building of early colonial churches. Much of the beauty of these graceful edifices is due to the skill and imagination of the Nahuas, who responded enthusiastically to the opportunity. The intricate roof decorations of Santa Maria Tonantzintla, which is close to Puebla, often referred to as the Rome of America because of its numerous churches, is a fine example. Decorated with polychrome and gold leaf and thickly adorned with angels, strange little animals, mysterious flowers and gorgeous fruit, it is a wonder to behold.

By the beginning of the 19th century, Mexico was the richest of all the overseas territories belonging to Spain, but as a colony she had become an anachronism. She was quite capable of self-government. Indian exploitation, resentment by the Creoles who were still not allowed to hold high office but were extremely wealthy from land ownership and mining, and the heavy taxation and export controls levied by the Spanish Crown, contributed to national unrest. Add to these ingredients other contemporary influences, with the breakaway of the 13 American colonies from Britain and the French Revolution, and we see that the time was becoming ripe for change. All these circumstances led to the establishment of independence in 1821.

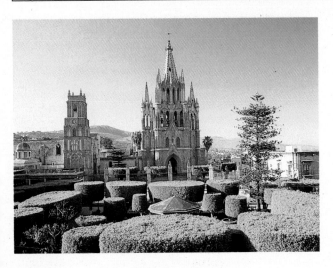

San Miguel de Allende was home to the Independence leader, Ignacio de Allende. It is a pretty town with an 18th-century character. In 1926 San Miguel was declared a national monument and today many citizens from Canada and the US retire here

Independence

The Mexican War of Independence can be said to have begun when the Spanish government discovered a revolutionary plot. This caused a parish priest Miguel Hidalgo, now considered father of the revolution, to ring his parish bell summoning his villagers to arms. Soon 50,000 Mexicans rallied to Hidalgo's call, but the priest did not turn out to be as good a soldier as he was a revolutionary, and instead of allowing his authority to come under the control of Ignacio Allende, a soldier, Hidalgo lead the battle strategy, with disastrous consequences. Finally, Hidalgo and Allende were betrayed and captured, and later executed for treason in Chihuahua.

However, by this time the torch of independence had caught alight and the final struggle began in 1820, when an outstanding officer, Agustín de Iturbide took over and finally established independence. Iturbide declared himself Agustín I, Emperor of Mexico; but pride came before the fall and soon afterwards he lost the support of the militia and was banished.

In 1822, the new republic came into being. The Monumento a la Independencia (Monument of National Independence) stands as tall as a lighthouse on the Paseo de la Reforma in

Mexico City, and if you cross the road to the island on which it stands you can see statues of the most outstanding heroes who were involved in the lengthy struggle.

During the early decades of the Republic, the government was badly served by its leaders. There was no firm policy and precious little continuity, as one leader after another was removed from power by unconstitutional methods. From the establishment of Independence until the Revolution in 1910, Mexico had 40 presidents and two emperors. In 1846, the United States declared war on Mexico, and Santa Anna, the general whose army won victory at the battle of the Alamo, was forced to cede about half of Mexico's territory, including California, Arizona and New Mexico, to the United States.

Soon afterwards, Mexico elected her first genuine statesman, a Zapotec called Benito Juárez, as her president. Today his statue can be seen in nearly every city throughout the country. When he took over his bankrupt country, he was forced to suspend payment on foreign debts, which led to problems with France, Britain and Spain. French troops invaded Mexico and put Archduke Maximilian on the throne as the new emperor. Benito Juárez fought for the survival of an independent Mexico for the next three years against Maximilian and the French. Then Napoleon III recalled his troops, leaving Maximilian to be captured by the Mexican army, and shot. Juárez was able to reduce the national debt, restore Mexican industry and commerce, bring about agricultural reform and improve human rights and education. A few years after Juárez died, Porfirio Díaz came to power and undid much of the good which Juárez had established. Without regard for human rights or democracy, he established a secret police force and re-instituted the *haciendas* at the expense of the Indians, now the poorest members of the population. Díaz ruled for 35 years before the Mexican Revolution ousted him in 1911.

From Revolution to the Present Day

Many prominent figures and charismatic heroes emerged during the Revolution, of which the best known were Emiliano Zapata and Francisco 'Pancho' Villa. After several years of turbulence, stability was restored, with a new constitution being drawn up in 1917 at Querétaro.

Politically, Mexico is now a well-established democracy, but for the last few decades there has been one ruling party, the Partido Revolucionario Institucional (PRI).

Recent years have seen progress in public welfare, including greater Social Security, the establishment of more schools and higher educational institutions, and an improvement in preventive medicine and health treatment.

Only five canals are left which pertained to the once famous city of Tenochtitlán, and all of them are in Xochimilco, where you can take a brightly painted gondola around the Floating Gardens. Along the way, other gondolas with romantic mariachi *and* marimba *bands will serenade you*

The mineral wealth of Mexico is enormous and the discovery of oil deposits in the Gulf has created a boom. Unfortunately, a decline in petroleum prices led to Mexico's foreign debts rising steeply.

President Zedillo's newly elected government (1994) has inherited the growing tension in Chiapas arising from exploitation of the indigenous people, and this, with subsequent devaluation of the peso has led to a recent downturn in Mexico's economy. Many of the big businesses involved in NAFTA (North American Free Trade Agreement) welcome the devaluation, but not the instability.

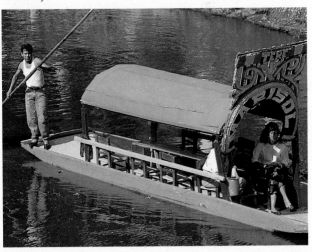

MEXICO CITY AND ITS ENVIRONS

Mexico City, the nation's capital, is located in the country's central highlands on a plateau 7,300 feet (2,225m) above sea level, and ringed by majestic, snow-covered volcanoes and mountains. Originally built on the shores of the now long-vanished Lake Texcoco, the city is land-locked. It is the largest metropolis in the world, a mass of wide boulevards, narrow streets, parks and gardens divided into *colonias*.

In the centre of the city is the **Plaza de la Constitución** (Constitution Square), often referred to as the **Zócalo**, and the largest city square in the Americas. Built on the site of the Aztec capital Tenochtitlán, it is surrounded by over 1,400 historical buildings, reflecting 300 years of colonial splendour when Mexico City was referred to as the 'city of palaces'. Taking up two sides of the square is the **Metropolitan Cathedral** which took 250 years to complete, and the **Palacio Nacional**, once the palace of Cortés, then the residence of the Spanish Viceroys and now the official residence of the president.

A 24-square-block area at the eastern end of **Bosque de Chapultepec** (Chapultepec Park), known as the **Zona Rosa** (the Pink Zone), houses most of the hotels as well as some of the country's best shops, restaurants, pavement cafés, pedestrian malls, art galleries and book shops. Nightlife is centred in bars, clubs and discos, and leading hotels arrange entertainment in the form of Mexican fiesta nights, with cabaret and dancing.

Paseo de la Reforma is the main artery of the city and was modelled by French architects on the style of the Champs-Elysées in Paris, at the behest of Emperor Maximilian. It runs from Plaza de la Constitución to the castle in Chapultepec Park, which he converted into his imperial residence and which is now open to visitors. The park, with its walkways, botanical gardens, large lake and zoo, is a favourite meeting place for Mexicans.

WHAT TO SEE

Castles, Palaces, Historic Mansions and Monuments

◆

CASA DE LOS AZULEJOS (HOUSE OF TILES)
Avenida Madero 4
Believed to have been built by the son of a Count of Valle de Orizaba. Told by his father he was an idle young man and would never be able to afford a house of tiles, the son changed his ways and then built this house from the wealth he earned, covering its façade with blue and white tiles. It now houses a restaurant, and artefacts are sold in the gallery.

◆◆◆

CASTILLO DE CHAPULTEPEC (CHAPULTEPEC CASTLE)
Chapultepec Park
Close to the entrance to the park, the castle was begun in 1795, and became the imperial palace of Maximilian, later

serving as a presidential home. In 1847 it was one of the last strongholds of the Mexicans during the United States invasion, stoutly defended by the Boy Heroes. The castle houses interesting carriages and the National Museum of History (see below).

◆
MONUMENTO A CUAUHTÉMOC (STATUE OF CUAUHTÉMOC)
Intersection of Paseo de la Reforma and Avenida Insurgentes Sur
Cuauhtémoc was the last Aztec emperor who fought against the Spaniards and is held in high regard and affection by the Mexicans. Depicted on the base are scenes from his life.

◆◆
MONUMENTO A LA INDEPENDENCIA (INDEPENDENCE COLUMN)
Paseo de la Reforma
Called *El Angel*, the golden figure on top of the 118-foot (36m) high column depicts the goddess of liberty. At the base are statues of famous citizens connected with the independence movement.

◆
PALACIO DE ITURBIDE (ITURBIDE PALACE)
Avenida Madero 17
Originally the imperial house of Agustín de Iturbide, who nominated himself Emperor Agustín I when he became ruler of independent Mexico in the 17th century. After losing the militia's backing Iturbide was banished in 1823 and having

El Angel *was erected to celebrate Mexico's struggle for independence*

failed in an attempted return to power, he was eventually executed by a firing squad. Today his palace, designed by the famous architect Francisco Guerrero y Torres, is owned by the National Bank of Mexico.

◆◆◆
PALACIO NACIONAL (THE NATIONAL PALACE) ✓
Plaza de la Constitución
On the eastern side of the Plaza known as the Zócalo, the Palace was built in 1692 on the site of the Palace of Moctezuma. It

houses the President's offices. Murals by Diego Rivera, at the top of the staircase and around the balcony on the first floor, colourfully present the history of Mexico. See the 'Freedom Bell', above the central balcony, which is rung on Independence Day by the President before a huge crowd. It comes from the town of Dolores Hidalgo and was rung by Father Miguel Hidalgo to summon village folk to his church at the start of the War of Independence in 1810. *Open*: daily: 07.00–19.00hrs.

PLAZA DE LAS TRES CULTURAS (PLAZA OF THE THREE CULTURES)

Unidad-Nonoako-Tlatelolco

The market square of old Tlatelolco, where the Aztecs fought their last battle against the army of Hernán Cortés. Seen here, representing three cultures, are the ruins of an Aztec ceremonial centre, a Spanish Colonial 16th-century church, and the contemporary Foreign Ministry building, all on the same plaza.

CENTRO DE LA CIUDAD DEL MÉXICO

Churches and Temples

◆◆◆
BASILÍCA DE GUADALUPE ✓

Calzada Misterios
Near Insurgentes Norte on the northern outskirts of the city, the basilica is built on the spot where the Virgin Mary is said to have appeared in 1531 before a lowly Indian called Juan Diego. It houses the most important religious painting in Mexico, and is a national shrine.

◆◆◆
CATEDRAL METROPOLITANA (METROPOLITAN CATHEDRAL)

Plaza de la Constitución Localo
It took 250 years to complete the cathedral, which was started in 1573 using many of the stones from the main temple of the Aztecs in Tenochtitlán. Within are 16 chapels and 21 altars. Note the twist in the main naves, due to the fact that the Spaniards filled in the Aztec canals and lake, and the foundations are now sinking.

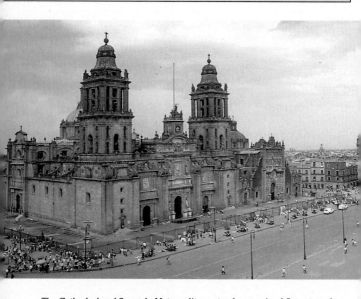

The Cathedral and Sagrado Metropolitano stand on a ruined Aztec temple

◆
IGLESIA DE JESÚS NAZARO Y HOSPITAL (JESUS OF NAZARETH CHURCH AND HOSPITAL)
República del Salvador and Pino Suárez

Three blocks south of the main square stands the house of Hernán Cortés, where a plaque commemorates his first meeting with Moctezuma. The hospital, founded in 1524, was the first to be built in Mexico, now completely renovated.

◆◆
TEMPLO MAYOR (GREAT TEMPLE)
Seminario

The ruins on the northeast side of the Metropolitan Cathedral were rediscovered in 1978. Quantities of artefacts were found, including an eight ton/tonne carved monolith to the moon goddess, now in the National Museum of Anthropology. Templo Mayor has its own Museum.

◆◆◆
TEOTIHUACÁN (CITY OF THE GODS) ✓

The ruins of this great city lie 30 miles (48km) northeast of Mexico City. Here is to be seen one of the finest Mesoamerican architectural sites in Mexico. Covering over eight square miles, the ruins are dominated by the great Pyramids of the Sun and Moon. It is best to go during the week, as residents of Mexico City crowd there at weekends. Sound and light shows take place from October to May.

Museums and Art Galleries

♦♦♦

BOSQUE DE CHAPULTEPEC (CHAPULTEPEC PARK)

Walking in the 'Forest of Grasshoppers' is a popular pastime, not only for visitors but also for residents of the city. On Sunday afternoons many local people picnic in this largest and oldest metropolitan park in the Americas. It contains eight museums, and three lakes, where you can take out a rowing boat. There is also a zoo and an amusement park. The zoo has 2,600 animals – over 300 species. It is a good place to take children, as there is a special area where they can get close to cubs and baby elephants as well as enjoy donkey rides and climb up tree houses.

♦♦

CIUDAD UNIVERSITARIA (UNIVERSITY CITY)

Cerro de Pedregal

Eight miles (13km) south of the Zócalo, the University's splendid wall murals and buildings, many of which incorporated Mesoamerican art forms, are well worth visiting, particularly for those interested in architecture.

♦♦

THE FLOATING GARDENS OF XOCHIMILCO

Xochimilco, some 15 miles (24km) southeast of the city centre

In Aztec times, when Mexico City was a waterborne city, rafts covered with soil were used to grow flowers and vegetables. In more recent times frameworks of sticks and clay were built in the lake shallows attached to the shore, and as the roots of the plants grew through the framework they anchored on the lake bottom, so forming the floating gardens. Today visitors travel through the remaining canals on colourful gondolas, while other boats carrying *mariachi* players and *taco* vendors float by. Weekend traffic is heavy.

♦♦

MUSEO DE BELLAS ARTES (MUSEUM OF FINE ARTS)

Avenida Juárez

Housed in the splendid Art Nouveau Palacio de Bellas Artes, which is also the name of the national theatre and opera and the famous Folklórico Ballet, the museum displays murals by famous Mexican artists: Camarena, O'Gorman, Orozco, Siqueiros and Tamayo. The second version of Rivera's *Man at the Crossroads* is here, the original of which was in the Rockefeller Centre before it was painted over because of its Marxist bias.

The palace, made of white Carrara marble, features a magnificent Tiffany glass mosaic curtain.

♦

MUSEO DE CERA (WAX MUSEUM)

Londres 6

Worth visiting for amusement. Usual formula of wax models of famous Mexicans and world history figures, plus a chamber of horrors, including Aztec human sacrifices.

MEXICO CITY AND ENVIRONS

◆◆
MUSEO DE LA CIUDAD DE MÉXICO (MEXICO CITY MUSEUM)
Pino Suárez 30

Prior to being rebuilt in the 18th century this manor belonged to the Counts of Santiago de Calimaya and dates back to 1528. Fine exhibits trace the history of Mexico City from pre-Columbian times to the present day.

◆◆
MUSEO FRANZ MAYER
Avenida Hidalgo 45, Plaza Santa Veracruz

The museum opened in 1986 in the beautifully restored 16th-century Hospital de Juan de Dios. It houses the private collection of Franz Mayer, a must for visitors interested in colonial decorative and applied arts.

◆◆◆
MUSEO NACIONAL DE ANTROPOLOGÍA (NATIONAL MUSEUM OF ANTHROPOLOGY ✓

Chapultepec Park

One of the finest exhibitions of its kind in the world. It is essential to visit prior to going on a classical tour. Provides a superb background history of Mesoamerica as well as housing great sculptures from the past. There are 25 rooms of exhibits (13 of archaeology and 12 devoted to ethnography). Multilingual guides are available, and there is an excellent bookshop.

◆◆
MUSEO NACIONAL DE ARTE (NATIONAL ART MUSEUM)
Tacuba 8

Near the main post office, the museum displays works of art by Mexican artists throughout history. Of particular significance is the fine bronze statue, by Manuel Tolsa, of *El Caballito*, the little horse that carried Charles IV of Spain.

This atlante is one of many magnificent statues in the National Museum of Anthropology

◆
MUSEO NACIONAL DE ARTE MODERNO (NATIONAL MUSEUM OF MODERN ART)
Chapultepec Park
The museum houses a permanent exhibition of the works of many of the great post-independence artists of Mexico.

◆◆
MUSEO NACIONAL DE ARTES Y INDUSTRIAS POPULARES (NATIONAL MUSEUM OF FOLK ART)
Avenida Juárez 44
Shows the best works of modern craftsmen and artists throughout Mexico. Housed in a former convent, you can purchase such items as glass and copperware, pottery and woven goods.

◆◆◆
MUSEO NACIONAL DE HISTORIA (NATIONAL MUSEUM OF HISTORY)
Chapultepec Castle, Chapultepec Park
Describes Mexico's history from the arrival of the conquistadores through to the Mexican Revolution. There are excellent murals by famous Mexican artists, including Juan O'Gorman, José Orozco and David Siquieros. Don't miss seeing the imperial apartments of Carlota and Maximilian, and the Gallery of Mexican History.

◆◆
MUSEO DE TEMPLO MAYOR (MUSEUM OF TEMPLO MAYOR)
Seminario
Opened in 1987, the museum has findings from the excavation of the Great Aztec Temple, and

This Rivera mural in the Palacio Nacional commemorates Aztec culture

is adjacent to the same site. It comprises eight halls devoted to Tenochtitlán's history from foundation to conquest. The most important display is of the Coyolxauhui Stone, representing the legend of the dismembered goddess.

◆◆
MUSEO TAMAYO (TAMAYO MUSEUM)
Paseo de la Reforma
In the park on the west side of the Reforma. Contains Tamayo's works, perhaps the doyen of Mexican modernists, plus those of other outstanding artists.

Accommodation

Mexico City offers everything from the ultra-modern, Super Deluxe hotels of the Zona Rosa or overlooking Chapultepec Park to small colonial-style hotels in less fashionable areas. Motels and guest houses are also in abundance. The price of hotels varies according to their standards. Because of sometimes quite rapid inflation it is best to check these prices before departure, but on the whole the Super Deluxe category of hotels may be 25 per cent lower in cost than its European equivalent. The classifications used are about equivalent to those in use in Europe and North America.

Super Deluxe

Camino Real (700 rooms) Mariano Escobedo 700 (tel: 203-2121).
Four Seasons (240 rooms) Paseo de la Reforma 500 (tel: 286-6020). This hotel arranges many interesting tours of Mexico City and its environs for guests.
María Isabel Sheraton (850 rooms) Paseo de la Reforma 325 (tel: 207-3933).
Nikko México (750 rooms) Campos Elíseos 204 (tel: 280-1111).

Moderate

The **Howard Johnson Gran Hotel** (124 rooms) Avenida 16 de Septiembre 82 (tel: 510-4040), is a charming, sophisticated and gracious hotel.
The **Marco Polo** (64 rooms) Amberes 27 (tel: 207-1893), is situated in the Zona Rosa's smartest street.
Other options include:
Aristos (360 rooms) Paseo de la Reforma 276 (tel: 211-0112) Zona Rosa.
Calinda Geneve (300 rooms) Londres 130 (tel: 211-0071) Zona Rosa.
Century (110 rooms) Liverpool at Amberes (tel: 726-9911) Zona Rosa.
Continental Plaza Aeropuerto (476 rooms) Fundidora Monterrey 89 (tel: 785-0505).
Fiesta Americana (616 rooms) Paseo de la Reforma 80 (tel: 705-1515).
Flamingos Plaza (256 rooms) Avenida de la Revolucíon 333 (tel: 627-0220).

Howard Johnson Gran Hotel is a masterpiece of art nouveau

Galeríe Plaza Westin (434 rooms) Corner of Hamburgo and Varsovia (tel: 230-1717) Zona Rosa.

Krystal Rosa (328 rooms) Liverpool 155 (tel: 211-0092) Zona Rosa.

Plaza Florencia (130 rooms) Florencia 61 (tel: 211-0064).

Presidente Inter-Continental (657 rooms) Campos Elíseos 218 (tel: 327-7000).

Ramada Aeropuerto (325 rooms) Boulevard Aeropuerto 502 (tel: 785-8522).

Reforma (300 rooms) Paseo de la Reforma and Paris (tel: 546-9687).

Ritz (125 rooms) Madero 30 (tel: 518-1340).

Royal (162 rooms) Amberes 78 (tel: 525-4850) Zona Rosa.

Sevilla Palace (414 rooms) Paseo de la Reforma 105 (tel: 705-2800).

Inexpensive

Bristol (150 rooms) Plaza Nacaxa 17 (tel: 533-6060).

Corinto (155 rooms) Vallerta 24 (tel: 566-9711).

Del Angel (100 rooms) Río Lerma 154 (tel: 533-1032).

El Diplomatico (107 rooms) Insurgentes Sur 1105 (tel: 563-6066).

El Ejecutivo (150 rooms) Viena 8 (tel: 566-6422).

María Cristina (146 rooms) Lerma 31 (tel: 566-9688).

Metropol (165 rooms) Luis Moya 39 (tel: 510-8660).

Prim (189 rooms) Versailles 46 (tel: 592-4600).

Plaza Reforma (104 rooms) Insurgentes Centro 149 (tel: 706-6111).

Vasco de Quiroga (50 rooms) Londres 15 (tel: 546-2614).

Economy

Catedral (116 rooms) Donceles 95 (tel: 518-5232).

Edison (45 rooms) Edison 106 (tel: 566-0933).

Fleming (75 rooms) Revillagigedo 35 (tel: 510-4530).

Hotel Canada (84 rooms) 5 de Mayo (tel: 518-2106).

Monte Carlo (59 rooms) Uruguay 69 (tel: 585-1222).

Markets and Craft Centres

There is a plentiful supply of interesting products to buy in Mexico (see **Shopping**, page 104).

Mexico City has innumerable places where craft stalls are set up, paintings are on display by local artists. The **Jardin del Arte**, at Parque Sullivan, Insurgentes and Reforma, is one such place where artists exhibit their work.

Among the leading craft centres are the **Mercado de la Merced** the biggest market in Mexico, which is to be found on Anillo de Circunvaluacíon.

The **Mercado de Artesanias de la Ciudad** at Balderas y Plaza Tres Guerra, where Mexicans shop, is one of the best and cheapest places to buy.

Bazaar Sábado at the Plaza San Jacinto-Villa Obregón in San Ángel is the place for high quality workmanship. It is open on Saturdays only.

Mercado de la Lagunilla on Calle Rayón sells absolutely everything. It is open on Saturday mornings.

El Artesanal Buenavista, behind the Buenavista railway station in a splendid building at Ayuntamiento 70, is another large market for handicrafts, including jewellery. These venues are very busy and colourful, and you are expected to haggle over the quoted cost.

Nightlife

Nearly all of Mexico City's larger hotels have night-clubs and many discotheques, hence a lot of the action is centred around the Zona Rosa (Pink Zone). About 22.00hrs is a good time to visit restaurants and dance spots, and most shows don't begin before midnight, despite what they might say on the programme. It is advisable to book in advance. Nearly all restaurants and night-clubs are closed on Sundays.

A good way to see some of the night spots outside of the hotels is to take a tour, which can be arranged at most hotel reception desks. These provide an opportunity to meet other people and to see what the city's nightlife has to offer – and it can also save you money.

If you want to explore, head for the Plaza de Garibaldi. It is here that the *mariachis* hang out – bands of musicians playing loud, exuberant music, dressed in traditional tight jackets, studded with silver buttons, and wide sombreros.

Discos start about 20.00hrs and finish around 04.00hrs, and usually have a cover charge around $10; drinks will be expensive. A cross section includes **Cero Cero** in Hotel Camino Real; **Disco Club 84** in the Presidente Hotel Chapultepec; **Lipstick** at the Hotel Aristos, on the Paseo de la Reforma 27; **La Cucarcha**,

Hamburgo 77 in the Zona Rosa; and **Zazzy** in the Nikko Hotel.

Theatre

Ballet Folklórico provides a rich tapestry of regional folk dances from all over Mexico. Music, costumes and choreography thrill the audience. Tickets can be purchased at the Belles Artes. For information (tel: 529-9320).

Night-clubs

Most shows take place twice nightly, at 23.00 and 01.00hrs. Below is a selection of some clubs:

Barbarella and **El Caballo Negro** night-clubs in the Paseo de la Reforma both feature top international stars nightly. **La Veranda**, also on La Reforma, does the same. Many of these night spots are to be found in leading hotels. After midnight the **Afro Tramonto** draws a crowd for its more risky show, at Insurgentes and Sullivan.

Night entertainment abounds in Mexico City. Fuller information and up-to-date prices can be obtained from a weekly publication called *Tiempo Libre*. New editions are available at newstands on Fridays.

Restaurants

There is a vast range of restaurants in Mexico City, many serving Mexican food and others specialising in different cuisines from around the world. A large number of restaurants feature a tourist menu at a nominal price which also includes a cocktail or wine. The downtown Centro Historico area is being renovated and many

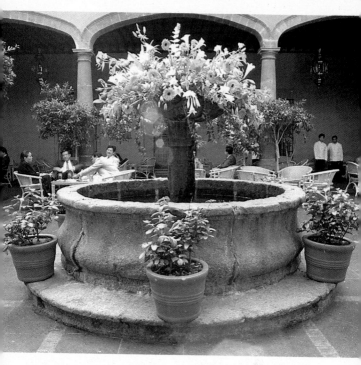

The flagstoned courtyard of an old hacienda is a cool and relaxing place to eat traditional food

majestic old buildings are being used for restaurants and shops. Hence it is worthwhile enquiring at your hotel desk for up-to-date information on where to eat out here. Mexicans eat their main meal at lunchtime and restaurants get busy around 14.00hrs, so if you want a leisurely meal and to avoid the rush, it's advisable to eat about 13.00hrs.

Top-of-the-range are the famous **Estoril** restaurants, international cuisine with Mexican flair, expensive but excellent. For the **Zona Rosa** restaurant (tel: 511-3421), for the **Pelanco** restaurant (tel: 531-4896). For

the best thoroughly Mexican food in the historic downtown centre try **El Centario**, again expensive but excellent (tel: 521-2934). **Fonda El Refugio**, over 40 years old, is internationally known for its Mexican cuisine. Situated in the Zona Rosa, it is not excessively expensive (tel: 528-5823). Good, inexpensive Mexican cooking in immaculately clean surroundings is to be found at **Las Cuezalas** in Rep de Columbia 69 (tel: 522-0689).

Sports and Activities

On Sundays bullfights or *Corrida*, take place in the world's largest bullring, **Plaza México**, on Insurgentes Sur (*Metro*: San Antonio - Line 7). Bullfights begin at 16.00hrs. Make sure you book a seat in the shade. The best time is December to March. Tickets from most hotel desks.

Rodeos, or *Charreada* are a popular activity for Mexicans and Charro associations arrange these usually on Sunday morning. Many are held at the **Rancho del Charro**, on the western side of Chapultepec Park, or at the **Lienzo del Charro** in Pedregal, on the south side of the city.

Soccer or *fútbol* enthusiasts will find this game has a huge following. Games usually take place at weekends throughout the year at the **Azteca Stadium** on the south side of the city (scene of the 1986 World Cup Final), the **Sports City Stadium** (Magdalena Mixuca) near the bullring and the **Olympic Stadium** in University City.

The longest racing season in the world is held at the **Hipódromo de las Américas** on Avenida Avila Camacho, and races start at 14.30hrs on weekends and at 15.00hrs on Tuesday, Thursday and Friday. Bets can be placed at under a dollar. You can dine at the Derby Club and watch the races at the same time.

One of the most exciting sports to watch is *jai alai*, the Basque variety of handball, which uses wicker basket gloves to hurtle the ball at breathtaking speeds. This can be seen every evening except Monday and Friday at the **Frontón México** on the Plaza de la República (*Metro*: Revolucíon - Line 2). Games begin about 19.00hrs, and the programme explains the finer points of the sport in English.

Transport

Mini-buses (*peseros*) are the cheapest above-ground method of getting around the city. They operate fixed routes and are indentified by destination plaques. Taxis are reasonably priced but at night the meters are not used. They display a *sitio* sign. Unmarked *turismo* limousines, usually outside hotels are useful for sightseeing and prices by the hour can be negotiated in advance.

Buses are cheap and depart from four outlying termini. The principal routes run along the Reforma, Juárez and Madero and from Chapultepec Park to Zócalo. The subway system (**Metro**) is one of the best anywhere and, again, fares cost only a few pesos. The stations are clean and well lit, some playing classical music, and colour-keyed signs define the different routes. Trains operate between 06.00hrs and midnight. Some forty **coach** tour operators run sightseeing tours around the city and to surrounding sites and the bigger hotels have information desks which can provide the visitor with useful data on places to see and times of coach departures. Toll road construction plans, such as the one connecting Mexico City to Acapulco, are rapidly improving ground transport in Mexico.

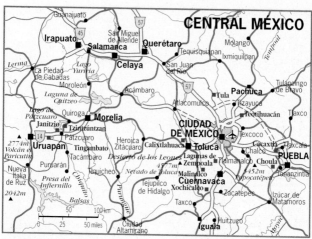

CENTRAL MEXICO

CUERNAVACA

Lying about 50 miles (80km) south of Mexico City is the capital of the state of Morelos. In Mesoamerican times the Indians called it Cuauhnáchuac, which to Spanish ears sounded like *cuerno de vaca* (cow's horn), and that is how the town came to be named. The altitude here is 2,000 feet (609m) lower than the capital and the temperature is balmy throughout the year. The Aztec nobility wintered here, Hernán Cortés built a palace, and Emperor Maximilian vacationed in an 18th-century mansion built by the silver magnate, José de la Borda. Today the tropical flowers and garden restaurants continue to attract the visitor away from the bustling crowds of Mexico City, either for the day or weekend. To purchase a variety of Mexican handicrafts, visit the Zócalo by the palace.

WHAT TO SEE

◆
CATHEDRAL
Avenida Hidalgo
Started in 1529 and hence one of the Old Mexican churches. Recently discovered murals depict scenes of martyrdom of missionaries who sailed to Japan in the 16th century.

◆
JARDÍN BORDA (BORDA GARDENS)
Built by a silver magnate of the same name, the magnificent mansion and gardens have been restored. Borda was fond of formal gardens and built numerous pools, fountains and terraces. There are frequent art exhibitions and concerts.

◆◆◆
PALACIO DE CORTÉS (PALACE OF CORTÉS)
Built by the Zócalo, the palace was begun in 1530 and today

The pyramid of Quetzalcoatl in Xochicalco shows the plumed serpent encircling the building and between the coils are sculptures of priests and astonomers

houses the **Museo de Cuauhnáhuac** (Museum of Cuauhnáhuac) which contains colonial furniture, historical exhibits and Diego Rivera murals recounting events in Mexican History.

◆
PYRAMID OF TEOPANZOLCO
Avenida Río Balsas
Near the railway station are the only Aztec remains in Cuernavaca.

◆◆◆
XOCHICALCO
A large defensible site handsomely restored, lying on the steep terraced hills of

Morelos, one hour's drive to the southwest of Cuernavaca.

Accommodation
Five minutes from the centre of Cuernavaca are three deluxe hotels: the colonial **Hosteria Las Quintas** (60 rooms) Boulevard Diaz 107 (tel: 18-3949); **Maximillian's** (60 rooms) Galeana 125 (tel: 18-2010); and **Del Prado** (204 rooms) Nardo 58 (tel: 17-4001).

Moderate
The **Posada Las Mañanitas**, at Ricardo Liñares 107 (tel: 12-4646) has tropical gardens where parrots, flamingos and peacocks are in residence. The facilities include an excellent dining room, cocktail lounge and heated swimming pool. The 38-room **Villa del Conquistador** at Paseo del Conquistador 134 (tel: 13-1166), has a splendid view of

Cuernavaca. As well as two restaurants and a bar with live entertainment, there are facilities for a variety of sports including swimming, squash, and miniature golf.
Others include:
Ejecutivo Inn (51 rooms) Coronel Ahumada 203 (tel: 16-0628).
Hacienda De Cortés (22 rooms) Plaza Kennedy 90 (tel: 17-3800).
Posada de Xochiquetzal (15 rooms) Calle Leyva 200 (tel: 18-5767).
Posada Jacarandas (90 rooms) Cuauhtémoc 805 (tel: 15-7777).
Racquet Club (52 rooms) Francisco Villa 100 (tel: 11-2400).

Inexpensive
OK Inn (46 rooms) Emiliano Zapata 825 (tel: 13-1270).
Palacio (16 rooms) Calle Morrow 204 (tel: 12-0553)
Papagayo (90 rooms) Motolinia 13 (tel: 14-1711).

Night-clubs
Cuernavaca is a lively place at weekends and nightspots are to be found in the Hacienda de Cocoyoc and the Hotel Casino de la Selva and there are several discos open at weekends which include **Barba Azul**, Prado 10, and **Maximiliano's**, Juan Ruiz de Alarcon 7.

Restaurants
Try **Restaurant Sumiya**, in Barbara Hutton's former Japanese-style residence, with its Zen contemplation pools designed by a Japanese priest from Kyoto.

La India Bonito Morrow is excellent for Mexican food at a reasonable price. For dining out in style there is **Le Château René**, Atzingo 11, and **Las Mañanitas**, Ricardo Liñares 107, with an international menu in a fine setting.

TAXCO

This oldest silver mining town in Mexico rests on the side of a mountain, some 50 miles (80km) to the southwest of Cuernavaca. The crooked streets of Colonial Taxco are paved with cobblestones, and nearly all the houses have red-tile roofs. 'Tlalco', the original name for the town means 'a place where they play'. The beautiful baroque church of Santa Prisca y San Sebastían dominates the centre, especially at night, when it is floodlit.
Taxco is full of shops selling well-crafted silver jewellery and *objets d'art*. If you are buying an expensive item, look for the hallmark – .925 – the government's requirement for purity in silver.

WHAT TO SEE

◆
CASA HUMBOLDT
Calle Juan Ruiz de Alarcón
It is a beautiful mansion, Moorish in design and originally an inn lying between the capital and Acapulco. It takes its name from the well-known 19th-century German traveller to these parts, Alexander Von Humboldt. Now sells interesting handicrafts from all over the state of Guerrero.

◆◆◆
IGLESIA DE SAN SEBASTIÁN Y SANTA PRISCA (CHURCH OF SANTA PRISCA)

The church has magnificent spires, a colourful dome and Churrigueresque style of interior which is the hallmark of 18th-century colonial architecture. Don't miss the fine paintings of Miguel Cabrera, one of the leading artists of this period.

◆
MUSEO GUILLERMO SPRATLING (SPRATLING MUSEUM)

Behind the main church is an exhibition of silver articles going back to the Mesoamerican period as well as models of colonial mines.

Accommodation

Moderate

Posada de la Misión on Avenida J F Kennedy (tel: 2-0063) is a converted old Spanish mission, decorated in colonial style. Most of its 150 rooms are on the small side, but there are some larger suites available. Facilities include a bar, disco, jacuzzi and tennis court and there is a fine Juan O'Gorman mural alongside the pool. Rates are moderate. Others include:

De la Borda (150 rooms) Cerro del Pedregal 2 (tel: 2-0025).
Hacienda del Solar (22 rooms) Off highway 95 south of town (tel: 2-0323).
Monte Taxco (188 rooms) Lomas de Taxco (tel: 2-1300).
Rancho Taxco-Victoria (147 rooms) Carlos J Nibbi 5 (tel: 2-1014).

Inexpensive

Los Arcos (tel: 2-1836) is just a stone's throw from the Zócalo, at Juan Ruiz de Alarcón 12. Its handsome, whitewashed rooms are situated round a cool courtyard and small fountain, and are reasonably priced. There is a small pool, piano bar, restaurant and rooftop terrace with a great view of the town. Others include:

Loma Linda (65 rooms) Avenida John F Kennedy 52 (tel: 2-0206).
Los Castillo (15 rooms) Juan Ruiz de Alarcón 3 (tel: 2-1396).
Santa Prisca (34 rooms) Cena Obscura 1 (tel: 2-0080).

Nightlife

Taxco's nightlife is fairly limited. Many café/restaurants overlook the cathedral and Plaza Borda. Among them are **Baio Paco** and **Bertha's**; the latter produces a mind-blowing Tequila and lime cocktail of the same name. Dancing can be found at **Windows** discothèque and **Tony Reyes'** at the Hotel Monte Taxco. On Saturday night there is a special fireworks display here. **Ventana de Taxco**, south of the town, is famous for its Italian dishes and gourmet cuisine.

PUEBLA

Puebla is two hours' drive southeast of Mexico City in the foothills of the Sierra Madre with several spectacular extinct volcanoes on its skyline. The town was built as a Spanish stronghold soon after the Conquest and it was here that a small Mexican army of 2,000 men defeated a French army three times its number. Its long

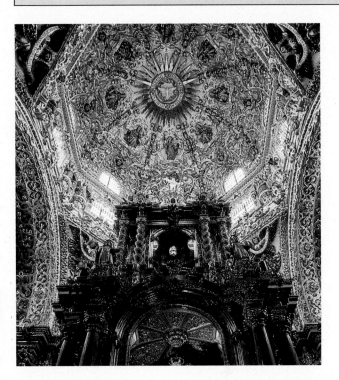

history as a ceramic centre dates back to pre-Columbian times and today it is often referred to as the 'City of Tiles'. You will see the use of hand-wrought Talavera tiles all over the city, on churches and administrative buildings and patios. You can buy tiles from the many factory shops.

WHAT TO SEE

◆◆◆
CATHEDRAL OF THE IMMACULATE CONCEPTION
on the Zócalo
The cathedral with the tallest towers in Mexico is notable for

Santo Domingo, Puebla, is among the best examples of Mexican baroque

its beautifully carved façade, fourteen chapels and its dome decorated with the local *azulejos* tiles.

◆◆
IGLESIA SANTO DOMINGO (CHURCH OF SANTO DOMINGO)
5 de Mayo
Dating from 1611, the church is worth seeing for its Rosary Chapel with its jewelled Virgin and walls of carved wood figures, gold leaf and tiles.

MUSEO AMPARO
Calle 2 Sur 708

A mansion housing interesting pre-Hispanic, colonial and vice-regal collections of Espinoza Amparo.

MUSEO DE ARTE JOSÉ LUIS BELLO Y GONZALEZ (BELLO MUSEUM)
3 Pontiente 302

The museum has interesting pictures by colonial artists as well as a collection of colonial furniture. Closed on Mondays.

PYRAMID OF CHOLULA
Five miles (8km) west of Puebla

Cholula became the most important city in the Valley of Mexico after the demise of Teotihuacán. The pyramid dedicated to Quetzalcóatl is the largest single structure in the Americas. It stands at 181 feet (55m) high and covers 40 acres (16 hectares). The site which has been influenced by Olmec, Teotihuacános and Toltec civilisations has been extensively excavated to expose stairs and plazas. Inside are miles of tunnels. Don't miss the colourful murals of the *bebedores*. The pyramid is partly covered by a 230-foot (70m) hill upon which stands the church, Nuestra Señora de los Remedios.

SANTA MARÍA TONANTZINTLA
Nine miles (14km) from Puebla

A marvellous example of how Indian artists interpreted Biblical teaching and their ability to adapt their art and skills from Mesoamerican architectural requirements to European.

Accommodation

Moderate
Generally considered to be the best place in town is **El Méson del Angel** at Avenida Hermanos Serdán 807 (tel: 24-3000). This 200-room hotel on the edge of town has landscaped grounds and good views of the volcanoes. Others include:
Aristos (120 rooms) Reforma and Calle 7 (tel: 32-0565).
Campestre Los Sauces (47 rooms) between Puebla and Cholula (tel: 47-1011).
Condado Plaza (68 rooms) Privada 6-B Sur (tel: 37-2733).
Gran Hotel Del Alba (208 rooms) Av Hermanos Serdán 141 (tel: 48-6055).

Inexpensive
The **Posada San Pedro**, at 2 Oriente 202 (tel: 46-5077), is a colonial-style hotel downtown with a small open-air swimming pool and two restaurants.
Other include:
Cabrera (60 rooms) 10 Oriente 6 (tel: 32-8525).
Gilfer (90 rooms) 2 Oriente 11 (tel: 46-0211).
Lastra (55 rooms) Calzada de los Fuertes 2633 (tel: 35-9755).
Palacio de Puebla (48 rooms) 2 Oriente 13 (tel: 42-4030).
Palacio San Leonardo (74 rooms) 2 Oriente 211 (tel: 46-0555).
Royalty (46 rooms) Portal Hidalgo 8 (tel: 42-4740).
Virrey de Mendoza (18 rooms) 3 Poniente 912 (tel: 42-3903).

Mole

Some culinary experts say that *mole*, the most famous spicy sauce in Mexican cooking, originated in the nun's kitchen at Santa Rosa. Its ingredients include chocolate, which is a Mesoamerican contribution to our diet, fresh and dried chilli, peanuts, almonds, cloves, cinnamon, tomato, onion and a host of vegetables, herbs and spices. *Mole* is traditionally served with chicken and turkey, and is to be found in restaurants all over Puebla, such as the **Hosteria de los Angeles** and **Fonda Santa Clara**, whose *mole poblano* is a favourite with the locals.

INDEPENDENCE ROUTE

In exploring the heart of Mexico, a worthwhile trip either privately by car or on a coach tour, is to follow the Independence Route that traces Mexico's struggle for liberty via Spanish colonial towns and villages on a 475-mile (764km) circular journey west and north of the capital.

QUERÉTARO

Lies two hours' drive north of the capital. It was taken over by the Spanish in 1531 and many beautiful churches were built here during the colonial period. It also became important during the fight for independence. Emperor Maximilian made his last stand here in 1867 and was executed by firing squad just north of town in the Cerro de la Campañas. It is also where Mexico's Constitution was prepared and signed. Together with nearby **Juan del Río** and **Tequisquiapan** (a thermal spa) the area has become the gem-cutting and polishing centre of Mexico, and here is the place to make your jewellery purchase.

Querétaro has beautiful colonial buildings set in parks and plazas

WHAT TO SEE

MUSEO REGIONAL DE QUERÉTARO (REGIONAL MUSEUM)

Juárez Street
Originally a 17th-century convent, it now contains colonial furniture including the table where Mexico had to sign away large territories west of the Mississippi after the Mexican War, plus other historical memorabilia.

◆◆◆
TULA ✓

Reached by Highway 57, which runs north from Mexico City to Querétaro. Most important Toltec site and former capital of that empire.

Accommodation

Moderate
Hacienda Jurica situated north of town, off Highway 57 (tel: 18-0022), is a 186-room hotel, built around a splendid 17th-century hacienda and offering a wide variety of facilities, including swimming, golf, tennis and horse riding. The **Real de Minas** on Constituyentes 124 Poniente, south of Highway 57 (tel: 16-0444), has over 200 comfortable rooms, each with wall-to-wall carpeting, air-conditioning, heating and TV. Among the hotel's other amenities are a piano bar, night club and private dining rooms.
Others include:
Holiday Inn (172 rooms) Av 5 de Febrero 110 (tel: 16-0202).
Méson de Santa Rosa (21 rooms) Pasteur Sur 17, Lapaza de Armas (tel: 14-5993).
Mirabel (171 rooms) Constituyentes 2 Oriente (tel: 14-3444).

Inexpensive
Azteca (45 rooms) Carr Querétaro – SLP (tel: 18-0016).
Hotel El Senorial (45 rooms) Guerrero Norte 10A (tel: 14-3700).

Restaurants
Many Querétaro restaurants can be discovered strolling down the Calle Corregidora, and some of the more up-market ones are to be found in hotels close to the Plaza Independencia. If you are keen on vegetarian food try the inexpensive **Comedor Vegetariano Natura**, part of a chain of four. If you are into steaks and shellfish, try the **Restaurante Josecho**, next to the Plaza de Toros Santa Maria.

SAN MIGUEL DE ALLENDE

One hour's drive further on from Querétaro is San Miguel de Allende, one of the few colonial towns designated a national monument and a favourite residential city for artists and writers from the USA who come to live in Mexico. Founded in 1542 by a Franciscan monk, Juan de San Miguel, 'Allende' was added in honour of the revolutionary Ignacio Allende who was born here. He fought beside Hidalgo for Independence. Six thousand feet (1,828m) up on the side of a mountain, this sleepy cobble-stoned colonial town with elegant

When the sun disappears at night its sail is said to be embodied in the jaguar, like this one at Tula

houses, and tree-lined patios is a great attraction to visitors. The main landmark is the Parroquía, a bizarre 19th-century Gothic church in pink stone, built by an illiterate stonemason who was inspired by postcards of European churches.

Accommodation

Moderate
The **Posada de la Aldea** at Ancha de San Antonio (tel: 2-1022), has 66 rooms, half overlooking a courtyard with a fountain.
Others include:
Aristos Parador San Miguel (60 rooms) Calle Ancha de San Antonio (tel: 2-0149).
Casa de Sierra Nevada (20 rooms) Hospicio 35 (tel: 2-0415).
Hacienda de las Flores (10 suites, 23 rooms) Hospicio 16 (tel: 2-1808).
Hacienda Taboada (70 rooms) Dolores Hidalgo Highway (tel: 2-0850).
Rancho el Atascadero (51 rooms) also bungalows, Prolongacíon Santo Domingo (tel: 2-0206).
Villas El Molino (50 rooms) Salida Real a Querétaro (tel: 2-1818).

Inexpensive
La Mansion del Bosque on Aldama 65 Juárez Parl (tel: 2-0277), is small, intimate and charming. The 24 rooms vary in size but are all tastefully furnished. Rates include breakfast and dinner.
Misíon de los Angeles (60 rooms) 1 mile (2km) along Hwy to Celaya (tel: 2-2099).

Economy

Méson de San Antonio (16 rooms) Mesones 80 (tel: 2-2897).

Posada Carmina (10 rooms) Cuña de Allende 7 (tel: 2-0458).

Posada las Monjas (63 rooms) Canal 37 (tel: 2-0171).

Posada San Francisco (40 rooms) Main Plaza (tel: 2-1466).

Quinta Loreto (38 rooms) Callejon de Loreto 15 (tel: 2-0042).

Sautto (25 rooms) Hernández Macias 59 (tel: 2-0052).

Restaurants

Entertainment is mainly found eating out in good restaurants such as **La Vendimia**, one of the city's best continental-style restaurants furnished in an artistic Mexican style, with flamenco songs sung by a lively guitarist. For good, reasonably priced pastas try the **Mama Mia**.

GUANAJUATO

An hour's drive from San Miguel, Guanajuato is situated in a canyon between two sierras at 6,700 feet (2,042m). It was a silver mining city and the **Valenciana Mine** here was one of the richest producing ever known. The cobble-stoned streets and stone steps amid churches and plazas are great for meandering. There is a unique underground subway for cars. Visit the **Jardín de la Uníon** (Garden of the Union), a favourite promenade plaza where band concerts are held. Nearby is the **Teatro Juárez** to which repertory companies, symphony orchestras and ballet

Painted houses and narrow crooked streets make Guanajuato attractive

schools from many different countries are invited. Near to the University, Diego Rivera, Mexico's greatest muralist, was born, and his house is now a **museum** which displays many of his early sketches and paintings.

Accommodation

Moderate

The striking **Posada Santa Fe** is located on the Jardín de la Unión (tel: 2-0084). It is a charming, colonial-style building which dates from the mid-19th century, and has a very popular outdoor café, though service here can be slow. The rooms are well kept and comfortable and rates are moderate.

Others include:
Castillo de Santa Cecilia (87 rooms) Subida a la Valencia s/n (tel: 2-0485).
Parador San Javier (117 rooms) Aldama 92 (tel: 2-0626).
Paseo de la Presa (60 rooms) Carretera Panoramica (tel: 2-3761).
Real de Minas (185 rooms) Nejayote 17 (tel: 2-1460).
San Gabriel Barrera Mision Park Plaza (162 rooms) Camino Antiguo a Maril Km 2.5 (tel: 2-3980).

Inexpensive
Posada San Francisco on Juárez at Gavira (tel: 2-2084), is across from the market, which can be noisy. The rooms are pleasant and rates are reasonable, but ask for a room in the interior, not off the balcony, as it will be quieter here.

Others include:
Del Conde (58 rooms) Insurgencia No 1 (tel: 2-1465).
El Insurgente (82 rooms) Av Juárez 224 (tel: 2-3192).
Guanajuato (50 rooms) Carr Guanajuato-Dolores Hidalgo Km 2.5 (tel: 2-0689).
Hacienda de Cobos (39 rooms) Padre Hidalgo (tel: 2-0143).
Hostería del Frayle (37 rooms) Sopeña 3 (tel: 2-1179).
Las Embajadoras (27 rooms) Parque Embajadoras (tel: 2-0081).
Mineral de Rayas (87 rooms) Calle Alhondiga No 7 (tel: 2-1967).
San Diego (43 rooms) Jardín de la Unión No 1 (tel: 2-1300).
Valenciana (35 rooms) Carr a la Valencia Km 2 (tel: 2-0799).
Villa de la Plata (57 rooms) Hwy 110 to Dolores Hidalgo (tel: 2-1173).

Restaurants
There is a great variety in terms of price and types of cuisine, mainly in the hotels themselves. **El Comedor Real** in the Hotel Castillo is in the top bracket, and **Tasca de Los Santos** is more moderately priced. Both give value for money.

MORELIA

Morelia is the capital of the state of Michoacán and you can now take a short flight or drive on new highways from Mexico City. The latter takes four hours. By and large most of the buildings belong to the traditional style of New Spain. The city was founded in 1541 by Antonio de Mendoza, the first viceroy, and originally called

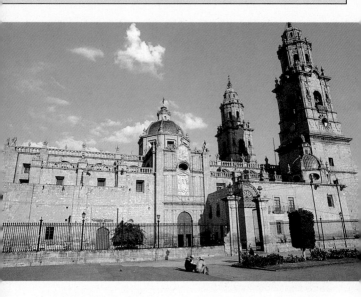

The dome of Morelia Cathedral is covered with ceramic tiles or azulejos

Valladolid. Its impressive **Cathedral** constructed of slightly pink stone, with its 200-foot (60m) tower, dominates the **Plaza de los Martires**. The majority of the city's leading attractions are within a six-block radius of this centre-piece, which took some 200 years to build.

Interesting places to see include the massive colonial **aqueduct** and the **Colegio de San Nicolás** (College of San Nicolas), the second oldest European educational institution in America. Morelia is noted for its lacquerware.

Accommodation

Moderate
The **Virrey de Mendoza** is conveniently located on the main plaza, at Portal de Matamoros 16 (tel: 12-0633). Originally a private house, this colonial-style hotel has over 50 bedrooms with soaring ceilings, hanging lamps and four-poster beds. It offers good food and service at a reasonable price.

Others include:
Alameda (116 rooms) Madero Poniente and Guillermo Prieto (tel: 12-2023).
Calinda Morelia Quality Inn (80 rooms) Av de la Carmelinas (tel: 15-7100).
Gran Hotel Centro de Convenciones (275 rooms) Av Ventura Puente (tel: 15-0023).
Posada de la Soledad (65 rooms) Zaragoza 90 (tel: 12-1888).
Presidente (90 rooms) Aquiles Serdan 647 (tel: 13-8080).

Real Victoria (111 rooms) Guadalupe Victoria 245 (tel: 13-2300).
Villa del Sol (102 rooms) Av Morelos Nte 1811 (tel: 12-4034).
Villa Montaña (40 rooms) Calle Patzimba (tel: 14-0231).

Inexpensive

The **Catedral** on Ignacio Zaragoza 37 (tel: 3-0783), is on the Zócalo. Its light and airy rooms, which are carpeted and have huge bathrooms, are arranged around a pleasant courtyard. Amenities include a café, restaurant and bar with live entertainment.
Others include:
Casino (50 rooms) Portal Hidalgo 229 (tel: 12-1252).

Restaurants

Most dining is in hotels or centrally located restaurants such as **Los Comensales** (tel: 12-9371), a moderately priced garden restaurant set in an old colonial house just north of the main plaza. Another good choice is the **Boca del Rio**, especially if you like fresh seafood (tel: 12-0374). If you prefer steak and poultry, try **El Rey Tacamba** on the north side of Plaza de Armas (tel: 12-9371).

PÁTZCUARO

Located 150 miles (241km) west of Mexico City at 7,000 feet (2,133m) above sea level and just a couple of miles from **Lago de Pátzcuaro** (Pátzcuaro Lake), the city of Pátzcuaro offers a relaxed atmosphere in a lovely setting and the opportunity to shop for a wide and interesting variety of crafts.

Pine forests and lakes make Pátzcuaro a very different place for travellers and vacationers who think of Mexico in terms of heat, sun and sand.
The main square is the **Plaza Vasco de Quiroga**, a peaceful courtyard surrounded by ash trees and colourful mansions. It is named after a 16th-century bishop. **Plaza Gertrudis Bocanegra** honours a heroine and martyr of Mexico's independence movement. Nearby is a library with a mural by Juan O'Gorman depicting the history of the Tarascan culture. The lake is 55 miles (88km) in circumference and contains a number of islands, including **Janítzio**, which is dominated by a giant statue in memory of José María Morelos, another hero of the independence movement. Friday is market day at the lakeshore, with vendors selling fried fish. Pátzcuaro whitefish and other lake fish are specialities of the area. About eight miles (12km) outside Pátzcuaro are the ruins of **Tzintzúntzan**. When the Spaniards arrived in this region, they estimated that 40,000 Tarascans lived in the city of temples, palaces and artisans' shops. The Tarascans were well known for their skill and artistry in metal work and jewellery. Friday is the main market day for crafts, but many shops are open every day. Pátzcuaro is noted for lacquerware, *rebozos*, *serapes*, sweaters, straw items, *huaraches*, copperware and hand woven fabric.
Some of the nearby villages specialise in different crafts, especially ceramics.

WHAT TO SEE

BASILÍCA DE NUESTRA SEÑORA DE LA SALUD (OUR LADY OF HEALTH)
Early colonial period with a revered 16th-century image of the Virgin made of corn paste.

ISLAND OF JANÍTZIO
Contains monolith of José María Morelos, larger than the Statue of Liberty.
Independence ceremony held here on the eve of 1 November.

MUSEO DE ARTES POPULARES (MUSEUM OF POPULAR ARTS)
Calle Alcantarillos
Houses a fine collection of ceramics, handicrafts, lacquerware and masks.

TINGAMBATO
On the road to Uruapan
A former Tarascan ceremonial complex with a pyramid, two plazas and a ballcourt.

◆◆◆
TZINTZÚNTZAN
Eight miles (12km) along main road to Quiroga
The original capital of the Tarascan Indians, called the 'place of the hummingbirds'. The archaeological ruins are distinctive and show five *yácatas*, or temple bases.

Accommodation

Moderate
Don Vosco (102 rooms) Av de las Américas 450 (tel: 2-0227).

Inexpensive
Mesón del Gallo at Dr José María Cross (tel: 2-1474), is an extremely well-maintained colonial mission-style hotel. The rooms are small but comfortable. Amenities include a pool and restaurant.
The **Posada de San Rafael** is on the main plaza at Plaza Vasco 18 (tel: 2-0770). It is a colonial-style inn with over 100 rooms surrounding a courtyard.
Others include:
Gran Hotel (26 rooms) Portal Regules 6 (tel: 2-0443).
Hosteria San Felipe (12 rooms) Lazaro Cardenas 321 (tel: 2-1298).
Los Escudos (30 rooms) Portal Hidalgo 73 (tel: 2-0138).
Mesón del Cortijo (14 rooms) Prolongacíon Alvaro Obregon (tel: 2-1295).
Misión San Manuel (42 rooms) Portal Aldama 12 (tel: 2-1313).
Posada de la Basílica (11 rooms) Arciga 6 (tel: 2-1108).

Economy
Valmen (17 rooms) Lloreda 34 (tel: 2-1161).

Restaurants
There is a selection of good restaurants serving excellent local dishes. Look out for *charales* and *boquerones* and for *trucha* (trout) which are caught in the lake. Restaurants are mainly located in the hotels or close to the two plazas.
Inexpensive local fish and local wine is available at **El Patio** (tel: 2-0484). **Restaurant Hotel Posada la Basílica** is open from 08.00–16.00hrs and is a good place to lunch on local dishes (tel: 2-1108).

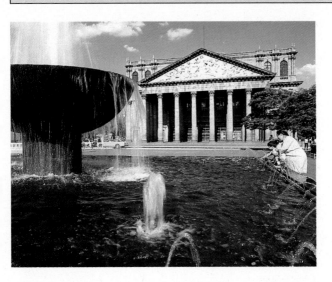

GUADALAJARA

Teatro Degollado in Guadalajara is modelled on Milan's La Scala

Guadalajara has a population of 3.5 million people and is the second largest city in Mexico. Located on a mile-high (1.6km) plateau some 360 miles (580km) north-west of Mexico City, it is known as the 'City of Roses'. Many Americans live here because of the ideal climate. Trees, flowers and fountains decorate the city. Founded in 1541, the centre of the city is a fine example of Spanish Colonial architecture and is dominated by the **Cathedral** which is surrounded by four plazas. Good shopping areas include, the **Mercado Libertad**, **Casa de Las Artesanías de Jalisco**, **Plaza del Sol** or the nearby villages of **Tlaquepaque** and **Tonalá**. The latter is the region's premier centre for ceramics, and attractive fauna and flora designs are displayed on traditional burnished pottery.

Of special interest is the **Teatro Degollado** (Degollado Theatre), with its vaulted ceiling decorated on themes from Dante's *Divine Comedy*. The work of the famous Mexican painter José Clemente Orozco figures prominently in Guadalajara. The **Palacio de Gobierno** (Government Palace) houses his masterpiece showing Hidalgo, the 'Father of Mexico's Independence', brandishing a fiery sword against a background of red flags and flames. In the **Hospico del Obispo Cabañas**, the artist has immortalised the Bishop Cabañas in the frescos with which he decorated the chapel; and more of his work is on display at **El Museo de Orozco**, where he lived and had his

studio and workshop.
Guadalajara's *Fiestas de Octobre*
is a month-long celebration
where international companies
perform symphony concerts,
opera and ballet. Other
attractions include rodeos,
bullfights, golf and tennis
tournaments. **Zona
Chapultepec**, with its centre
walkway festooned with trees
and fountains, boutiques, art
galleries, haute cuisine
restaurants, cafés and
bookshops, is Guadalajara's own
Zona Rosa.

WHAT TO SEE

◆◆◆
BARRANCA DE OBLATOS
*11 miles (17km) along Calzada
Independencia*
A 2,000-foot (630m) canyon, that
has been cut out in geological
time by two rivers. A cable car
descends to the canyon floor

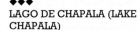
*Guadalajara can best be seen from
the tall towers of the Cathedral*

with its hot springs and lush
vegetation.

◆◆
CATHEDRAL
Plaza de Los Laureles
The cathedral was started in
1571 and displays several styles
of architecture, including Gothic,
baroque and Renaissance. Note
the *Assumption of the Virgin* by
Murillo by the entrance to the
sacristy.

◆◆◆
LAGO DE CHAPALA (LAKE
CHAPALA)
One hour south of Guadalajara
and popular for one day
excursions, the lake was named
after a Taltica Indian chief. This is
the largest lake in Mexico. On its
shoreline is the pleasant resort of
the same name. A popular

meeting place is the Beer Garden at the end of the main street. Launches can be rented for a tour of the lake.

◆
MUSEO DEL ESTADO DE JALISCO (REGIONAL MUSEUM)

Next to the cathedral the museum has a large display of pre-Hispanic historic memorabilia.

◆◆◆
TEATRO DEGOLLADO ✓

Plaza de la Liberacíon
Its vaulted ceiling is decorated on themes from Dante's *Divine Comedy*, and it has regular performances by the University of Guadalajara's folk ballet troupe as well as plays and concerts.

Accommodation

Moderate
The **Frances** is just off Plaza de la Liberacíon, at Maestranza 35 (tel: 613-1190). It is the oldest hotel in Guadalajara, and is now a designated national monument. The rooms are pleasant – try to get one looking out on the Palacio de Gobierno – and there is a restaurant with live music and dancing. Rates are very reasonable.
The **Lafayette** at Avenida La Paz 2055 (tel: 615-0252), is in the heart of the financial district and close to the airport. Its 200 rooms have air conditioning, colour TVs and telephones.

Lake Chapala is Mexico's largest inland lake. Make sure fish caught in these waters is well cooked

Prices are moderate and it is conveniently situated near the city's night clubs and best restaurants.
Others include:
Aranzazu (500 rooms) Revolucíon and Degollado (tel: 613-3232).
Calinda Roma (176 rooms) Juárez No 170 (tel: 614-8650).
Camino Real (210 rooms) Av Vallarta 5005 (tel: 647-8000).
Carlton Hotel Guadalajara (222 rooms) Av Niños Héroes y de 16 Septiembre (tel: 614-7272).
De Mendoza (104 rooms) V Carranza No 16 (tel: 613-4646).
El Tapatío (114 rooms) Blvd Aeropuerto 4275 (tel: 635-6050).
Fiesta Americana (414 rooms) Aurelio Aceves 225 (tel: 825-3434).
Holiday Inn Crowne Plaza (305 rooms) López Mateos and Mariano Otero (tel: 634-1034).
Hyatt Regency Guadaljara (420 rooms) Av López Mateos (tel: 122-7778).
Plaza Reyes (171 rooms) Calzada Independencia Sur 164 (tel: 613-8513).
Plaza del Sol (352 rooms) López Mateos Sur (tel: 647-8790).

Inexpensive
Canada (125 rooms) Estadio 77 (tel: 619-4014).
Chapalita (79 rooms) López Mateos 1617 (tel: 621-0607).
Colón (100 rooms) Ave Revolucíon Poniente No 12 (tel: 613-3390).
Del Bosque (73 rooms) López Mateos 265 (tel: 621-4650).
Del Parque (100 rooms) Juárez 845 (tel: 625-2800).
Fenix (206 rooms) Corona 160 (tel: 614-5714).

Guadalajara (68 rooms) Vallarta 3305 (tel: 647-8489).
Internacional (112 rooms) Pedro Moreno 570 (tel: 613-0330).
La Estancia Del Sol (64 rooms) Mariano Otero 2407 (tel: 631-6164).
Nueva Galicia (100 rooms) Corona 610 (tel: 614-8780).
Palacio (135 rooms) Calz del Ejército (tel: 619-9262).
Plaza Diana (200 rooms) Augustín Yánez 2760 (tel: 615-5510).
Plaza Genova (197 rooms) Juárez 123 (tel: 613-7500).
Posada del Sol (54 rooms) López Mateos Sol 4205 (tel: 631-5205).
Posada Guadalajara (170 rooms) López Mateos Sur 1280 (tel: 621-2022).
Posada Virreyes (60 rooms) On highway to Mexico City (tel: 635-0155).
Universo (137 rooms) López Cotilla 161 (tel: 613-4372).

Restaurants
For expensive haute cuisine try the **Place de la Concorde** in the Hotel Fiesta Americana. For traditional local dishes with a creole influence in classical Mexican surroundings visit **La Vianda**, Av Chapalita 120. Guadalajara has a good choice of restaurants to suit all budgets.

Nightlife
All-night dancing can be enjoyed at several discos, such as **Daddy-O** (on Av López Mateos and Atzayacatl) and at **Oz** (on Av López Mateos and Mariano Otero). Nightclubs are found in many of the major hotels, usually with cabaret.

The beautiful bay of Acapulco is fringed with deluxe hotels

RESORTS ON THE PACIFIC COAST

Of the three bodies of sea that surround Mexico, the Gulf, the Caribbean and the Pacific, apart from Cancún the most popular resorts are to be found on the Pacific. South from Mazatlán are 2,000 miles (3,218km) of spectacular and varied beaches. This area is in a state of continual development and improvement, although as the development of the coastline has moved in a southerly direction, you will find the more traditional resorts are along the northern shores. Set out below are some of the coastal playground venues which attract the visitors for beach holidays, fishing and golf.

ACAPULCO

The luxury high-rise hotels which line 20 or more sun-drenched beaches and glittering Acapulco Bay attract the jet-set and holiday makers from all over the world. The centre of town, often referred to as 'traditional' Acapulco, lies on the western side of the Bay. The most popular beaches are in this area. **Playa Condesa** is the most frequented, but there are over 20 more, each fulfilling a different need (there are 'morning beaches', 'afternoon beaches', swimming and sporting beaches).

The Strip from the Exelaris Hyatt Regency to the Acapulco Paraiso is where the nightlife, restaurants and high class shops

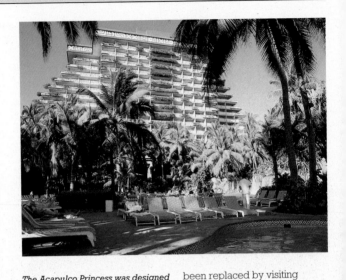

The Acapulco Princess was designed to resemble an Aztec pyramid

are to be found. On the mountain road, overlooking the surrounding bay, **Las Brisas**, with a host of villas, each with its own swimming pool, offers the privacy, luxury and service which has made it one of the most famous honeymoon complexes in the Americas. Along **Playa Revolcadero**, between the town centre and the airport, is the famous **Acapulco Princess**, built on the style of an ancient Mexican pyramid, and its sister hotel, the **Pierre Marqués**, originally built by Paul Getty as his own special hideaway. Both hotels feature golfing packages, with a choice of 18-hole championship courses.

Once Acapulco was the main port-of-call for ships laden with ivory, porcelain and silk from the Orient. Today, these have been replaced by visiting cruises ship and the *tianquis* or market place, has now become a major conference centre. Hotels range from inexpensive to deluxe and among the leading international hotel chains with properties here are Hyatt, Sheraton Princess, Quality Inn and Presidentes. Every kind of water sport is catered for along with tennis and golf. There are also a great variety of cruises, many with entertainment on board. Don't miss the high divers at **La Quebrada**. They dive at night time, by torchlight from a 135-foot (41m) escarpment into shallow rock pools.

Buses run regularly, virtually from one end of the Bay to the other, while an ocean-side promenade (*malecón*) edges the city's activity. West of the city, **Pie de la Cuesta**, is the best beach for watching Acapulco's spectacular sunsets.

WHAT TO SEE

SAN DIEGO FORT

The 17th-century fort overlooks the cruise ship pier, and houses pre-Hispanic relics and other historical memorabilia pertaining to the State of Guerrero.

LAGUNA DE COYUCA

West of the city, near the beach of Pie de la Cuesta

This is a freshwater lagoon and bird sanctuary enclaved by coconut palms, where you can swim or fish. The lagoon can be reached by canoe or rowboat, which can be hired at Pie de la Cuesta.

CENTERO INTERNATIONAL

An amusement park for children featuring dolphin and seal shows, it also offers plays, symphony concerts and ballet during much of the year. Special performances can be seen on the billboard in front by the Costera.

PIE DE LA CUESTA

Seven miles (12km) northwest of Acapulco

A village on a sandbar by the Laguna de Coya, with boating and swimming facilities. Beautiful sunsets, birds and flowers. Seafood restaurants and *mariachis* a speciality.

Accommodation

Super Deluxe

The **Hyatt Regency** (592 rooms) Costera Miguel Alemán No 1 tel: 84-2888), is located directly on Acapulco's Bay.
Acapulco Plaza (1,000 rooms) Apartado Postal C-88, Costera Miguel Alemán 123 (tel: 85-8050).
Acapulco Princess (1,031 rooms) Playa Revolcadero, Apartado Postal 1351 (tel: 69-1000).
Las Brisas (265 casitas) Apartado Postal 281, Carretera Escenica 5255 (tel: 84-1580).
Pierre Marqués (340 rooms) Playa Revolcadero, Apartado Postal 474 (tel: 84-2000).
Villa Vera Hotel and Racquet Club (80 villas) Apartado Postal 260 (tel: 84-0333).

Moderate

Plaza Las Glorias Mirador (130 rooms) at La Quebrada 74 (tel: 83-1155), is the place to watch Acapulco's famous cliff divers.
Acapulco Ritz (253 rooms) Costera Miguel Alemán (tel: 85-7544).
Acapulco Tortuga (250 rooms) Costera Miguel Alemán 312 (tel: 84-8889).
Club Majestic (185 rooms) Pozo del Rey 73 (tel: 83-4710).
Copacabana (432 rooms) Tabachines 2 (tel: 84-3260).
Elcano Royal (180 rooms) Av de las Palmas and del Parque (tel: 64-1950).
El Presidente (146 rooms) Apartado Postal 933, Costera Miguel Alemán (tel: 84-1700).
El Tropicano (137 rooms) Costera Miguel Alemán 510 (tel: 84-1332).
Howard Johnson Maralisa (90 rooms) Costera Miguel Alemán (tel: 85-6677).
La Palapa (324 suites) Fragata Yucatán 210 (tel: 84-5363).

Las Hamacas (160 rooms) Costera Miguel Alemán (tel: 82-4768).
Marbella (43 rooms) Horacio Nelson 2 (tel: 84-2890).
Maris (84 rooms) Costera Miguel Alemán (tel: 85-8492).
Panoramic (200 rooms) Av Condesa 1 (tel: 84-0724).
Plaza las Glorias Paraiso (422 rooms) Costeria Miguel Alemán 163 (tel: 85-5596).

Inexpensive
Arbela (50 rooms) Costera Miguel Alemán 55 (tel: 84-2165).
Autotel Ritz (103 rooms) Costera Miguel Alemán (tel: 85-8023).
Belmar (80 rooms) Gran Via Tropical (tel: 83-8098).
Casa Blanca (120 rooms) Cerro de la Pinzona (tel: 82-1212).
De Gante (143 rooms) Costera Miguel Alemán 265 (tel: 85-0232).
Los Flamingos (47 rooms) Av López Mateos (tel: 82-0690).
Siete Mares (50 rooms) Pozo del Rey s/n (tel: 83-1118).
Vilia (60 rooms) Av Roqueta 154 (tel: 83-3311).
Also available are a plethora of reasonably priced self-catering condominiums and villas to rent.

Restaurants
Restaurants abound, offering everything from inexpensive local dishes to haute cuisine. Seafood is a speciality. Two good places to sample great seafood are **Beto's** on Condesa Beach, with a very lively atmosphere and **Pipo's** just off the Costera, where the food is excellent and very reasonably priced. There is also a big selection of discos, roof-top supper clubs with dancing and night clubs with shows.

Nightlife
The choice of venues is so large and varied it is advisable to discuss the choice and prices with your hotel information desk, or get the Acapulco tourist board's publication *The Difference is Night and Day*.

IXTAPA/ZIHUATANEJO

By car, this relatively new, two-town, world class resort, is only 3½ hours drive from Acapulco and now has its own international airport. Once little more than the home of a few fisher folk, these scenic bays at the base of the Sierra Madre are popular venues for those who like to live less formally than in Acapulco.
Considerable effort and care by the Mexican government has gone into opening up this area to visitors, while at the same time successfully retaining the natural beauty and unspoilt coastline.
Sportsmen will enjoy a great variety of watersport, and there is an excellent golf course at the **Palma Real Golf and Tennis Club** in Ixtapa.
One of the main attractions is nearby **Ixtapa Island**, which has a wildlife reserve and offers excellent snorkelling and diving. Fishermen will find in the waters around Zihuatanejo, just a few miles/km south of Ixtapa, an abundance of fish, including sailfish, marlin, roosterfish, yellowtail and bonito. Gear, bait and boats can be hired at the pier in Zihuatanejo. Boats also

go out with parties who wish to snorkel and scuba dive, or there are moonlight cruises which can be booked in advance.

Accommodation

Super Deluxe
The **Dorado Pacifico** situated at Palmar Bay (tel: 3-2025), is one of Ixtapa's nicest hotels. It has 285 pleasant, spacious rooms with balconies and amenities include a large pool with swim-up bar, tennis courts and parasailing.
Club Méditerranée (375 rooms) Playa Quieta (tel: 3-0924).
Westin Brisas (428 rooms) Playa Vista Hermosa (tel: 3-2121).

Moderate
Aristos (226 rooms) Blvd Ixtapa (tel: 3-0011).
Castel Palmar (110 rooms) Palmar Bay (tel: 4-2341).
Holiday Inn Sunspree (195 rooms) Blvd Ixtapa (tel: 3-1066).

Krystal (302 rooms) Blvd Ixtapa (tel: 3-0333).
Presidente (400 rooms) Blvd Ixtapa (tel: 3-0018).
Sheraton Ixtapa (358 rooms) Av Ixtapa (tel: 3-1858).

Inexpensive
Alva (27 rooms) Juan N Alvarez (tel: 4-2010).
Posada Caracol (55 rooms) Playa La Madera (tel: 4-0235).
Riconado del Hujal (24 rooms) Paseo de los Hujes (tel: 4-2071).
Solimar Inn (14 rooms) Plaza los Faroles (tel: 4-3692).
Zihuatanejo Centro (70 rooms) Augustín Ramírez 2 (tel: 4-3661).

MANZANILLO

Situated at the Costa de Oro, Manzanillo is a major port with excellent beaches, surrounded by jungle and fruit plantations; good for watersports and a

This beach at Zihuatanejo is part of Mexico's 6,212 miles (9,997km) of golden coastline

centre for spectacular sea fishing. It lies about midway along the Mexican coastline, some nine hours drive northwest of Acapulco. An important annual deep-sea fishing tournament takes place in February. The port city is often referred to, in angling circles, as the sailfish capital of the world. Railway lines pass through the city to the docklands where freighters and naval ships tie up. Nearby, in the small harbour, fishing boats are for hire. The La Mantarraya 18-hole golf course at Las Hadas has been rated by 'Golf Digest' to be among the 100 best courses in the world. Beyond the port, Manzanillo has many fine beaches where tourist accommodation is improving every year. **Playa Azul**, just around the bay, is a seven mile (11km) long beach lined with hotels, while the smaller **Playa Las Brisas** is a little further on. Sixty-one miles (98km) inland to the east is **Colima**, the provincial capital, with simple colonial buildings. Also in the region is the active volcano **Nevado de Colima**.

Accommodation
Accommodation is available to suit all pockets and the super deluxe **Las Hadas Hotel**, where Dudley Moore and Bo Derek frolicked in the film *10*, has its own yacht marina.

Super Deluxe
Las Hadas (220 rooms) Av de los Riscos y Vista Hermosa s/n (tel: 4-2000).
Sierra Radisson, (350 rooms) Plaza Audencia 1 (tel: 3-200).

Moderate
Club Maeva (514 rooms) Bahia de Santiago s/n (tel: 5-0595).
Club Santiago (137 rooms) Carrizales s/n Bahia de Santiago (tel: 5-0413).
Costa Real (56 rooms) Santo Domingo 1 (tel: 3-0725).
Fiesta Mexicana (200 rooms) Carr Manzanillo-Santiago Km 8.5 (tel: 3-2180).
La Posada (24 rooms) Calz Gral Lazaro Cardenas 201 (tel: 3-1899).
Playa del Oro (300 rooms) Carr Manzanillo-Cihuatlán (tel: 3-1870).
Playa de Santiago (105 rooms) Balneario de Santiago s/n (tel: 3-0055).

Inexpensive
The **Colonial**, Avenida Mexico 100 (tel: 2-1080) in downtown Manzanillo is an unpretentious colonial-style hotel.
Also: **Las Brisas** (57 rooms) Av Lazaro Cardenas (tel: 3-2075).

Economy
Nuevo Hotel Anita (50 rooms) Playa de Santiago (tel: 3-0161).

Nightlife
Fairly limited in this area, but lively discos do exist, for example, **Oui** and **Enjoy** on the Santiago/Manzanillo road. At **Bugatti's** dancing to a piano goes on to the early hours. Also at **Lagazpi**.

Restaurants
A good variety, ranging from places like **El Vaquero** which serves Hereford beef Monterrey style, to places with delicious seafood such as **Ostería Bugatti**.

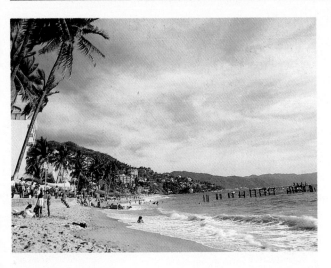

PUERTO VALLARTA

Twenty years ago Puerto Vallarta was only a sleepy fishing village!

Puerto Vallarta rests on Bahía de Banderas (the Bay of Banderas) some 175 miles (282km) north of Manzanillo. This bay is the largest natural bay in Mexico with many miles of coastline ringed by mountains. It was a sleepy fishing village until Richard Burton and Elizabeth Taylor made the film *Night of the Iguana* here in the 1960s. Since then this quaint town with its cobble-stoned streets, colonial-style street lighting, and pastel-coloured buildings, often decorated with bougainvillea, has become a popular seaside resort. Puerto Vallarta is now a modern resort offering a wide range of activities, which include waterskiing, windsurfing, sailing. parasailing, riding, tennis and golf. **Playa del Sol** is the most popular beach. Several large yachts provide half-day and full day cruises around the Bay, stopping off at the **Yelapa beach**, whose name means 'meeting place'. Between mid-May and early June is the main city fiesta with bullfights, *charredas* (rodeos), carnival floats and all manner of Mexican entertainment. A ferry service runs between Puerto Vallarta and **Cabo San Lucas** at the tip of Baja California: the crossing takes around 18 hours. Economic transport buses run between the airport and hotels.

WHAT TO SEE

◆
ISLA RÍO CUALE
The Río (river) Cuale, picturesque in its upper stretches, separates into two arms just before passing into the sea. The river encircles an island in the centre of Puerta

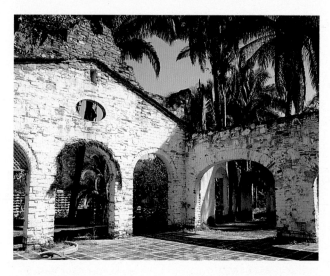

Vallarta, on which is a small museum, craft shops, open-air cafés and a children's playground.

◆◆
LOS ARCOS
To the south of town, Los Arcos are rock formations lying about 1,650 feet (500m) offshore, having been carved out by pounding waves. They can be seen from any southbound car, bus or boat.

Accommodation

Super Deluxe
Continental Plaza (425 rooms) Av de las Garzas (tel: 4-0123).
Fiesta Americana (219 rooms) Av Francisco Medina Km 2.5 (tel: 4-2010).
Plaza las Glorias (390 rooms) Av de las Garzas (tel: 4-4444).
Presidente Inter-Continental (120 rooms) Carr Barra de

Ruins of the film set from 'Night of the Iguana', Puerto Vallarta

Navidad Km 8.5 (tel: 3-0507).
Ramada Vallarta (470 rooms) Carr Aeropuerto Km 3.5 (tel: 4-1700).
Sheraton Buganvilias (670 rooms) Carr Aeropuerto 999 (tel: 3-0404).
Westin Regina Vallarta (280 rooms) Paseo de la Marina 205 (tel: 1-1100).

Moderate
Buenaventura (210 rooms) Av México No 1301, Cuale North (tel: 2-3737).
Conchas Chinas (340 rooms) Carr Barra de Navidad Km 2.5 (tel: 4-1010).
Krystal Vallarta (432 rooms) Av de las Garzas s/n (tel: 4-0202).
Las Palmas (147 rooms) Paseo de las Palmas Km 2.5 (tel: 4-0650).
Molino de Agua (53 rooms)

Vallarta 130, Ignacio (tel: 2-1956).
Pelicanos (190 rooms) Av Francisco Medina Km 2.5 (tel: 4-1010).
Playa del Oro (400 rooms) Av de las Garzas 1 (tel: 4-6868).
Playa Los Arcos (145 rooms) Olas Atlas 380 (tel: 2-0583).
Vacation Club Vallarta (48 rooms) Morelos y Libertad (tel: 2-1152).

Inexpensive
Costa del Sol (48 rooms) Carr Aeropuerto Km 1 (tel: 2-2055).
Eloisa (149 rooms) Lázaro Cárdenas 179 (tel: 2-1500).
Encino (75 rooms) Juárez 122 (tel: 2-0051).
Posada del Angel (50 rooms) Carr Aeropuerto Km 1.5 (tel: 4-1229).
Posada de Roger (50 rooms) Basilio Badillo 237 (tel: 2-0839).
Tropicana (249 rooms) Amapas 274 (tel: 2-0829).

Restaurants, Discos and Night Clubs
These are in such plentiful supply that the visitor is spoilt for choice.
The award-winning chef at **La Perla** restaurant offers the best in French nouvelle cuisine at the Hotel Camino Real.

MAZATLÁN

Mazatlán, or 'Place of the Deer', lies on a rocky promontory opposite the tip of Baja California and has a ferry service to **La Paz** on this peninsula (crossing time, 16 hours). The nation's largest shrimp fleet and the finest harbour facilities of Mexico's Pacific coast are found here. Marlin and sailfish are caught in great quantities year round and eight fleets of charter boats are on call to take fishermen out. Situated on a headland, there is a choice of beaches, some have evocative names; **Las Gaviiotas** (the Seagulls), is the beach nearest town, further north, **Playa Sabalo** is the best of Mazatlán's beaches while the island beach of **Vendos** offers exceptionally clear and calm waters. The big rollers on some of the beaches attract surfing enthusiasts. Hunting for everything from mountain lion to wild boar is also available. Every year three major events take place here. The **Carnival**, which some say is the best in the world after Río de Janeiro and New Orleans occurs between Friday and Tuesday before Lent. Accommodation for this event gets booked out six months in advance. The second is the opening of the fishing season when the Bishop of Mazatlán leads a procession down to the dock to bless the fleet. This takes place on 15 September. The third is the Mazatlán Fishing Tournament at the end of August, beginning of September.
After sundown, the palm-fringed and brightly-lit **Malecón** becomes a veritable ocean-side *paseo*, alive with strollers and passing vehicles of all descriptions, including four-wheel carriages, three-wheeled taxis and *arañas* (covered carts). A new development creating a yacht basin with dry dock facilities and 1,000 berths, along

PACIFIC COAST RESORTS – MAZATLÁN

Surfing on huge Pacific rollers and sea fishing are popular in Mazatlán

with other tourism infrastructure, including a 27-hole golf course, hotels and shopping centres is under construction, and some of these facilities are now available. This Marina Mazatlán will soon be attracting yacht owners from all over the world.

WHAT TO SEE

EL FARO
Situated on **Cerro del Crestón** the promontory separating the port from the ocean, is El Faro – one of the tallest lighthouses in the world.

EL MIRADOR
Intersection of Paseo Claussen and Olas Atlas
Once a lookout tower, now twice each day daredevil young divers plunge from the top into the sea below. Not as spectacular as the high diving in Acapulco, but dangerous nonetheless.

Accommodation

Super Deluxe
The **Marina El Cid Hotel and Yacht Club** is a complex of different pastel-coloured luxury villas, built in a Mediterranean style, which forms an arc around the yacht marina and swimming pool. There are some 200 self-contained suites.

Moderate
The **Suites Las Flores** (119 rooms) Loaiza 212 (tel: 13-5100), on the beach, is a high-rise hotel offering apartments with kitchens, ideal for a longer stay, as well as standard rooms. The atmosphere is easy-going and relaxed, though its popular bar and beachfront can become very lively.

Aqua Marina Best Western (101 rooms) Av del Mar 110 (tel: 81-7080).
Belmar (132 rooms) Olas Atlas Sur 166 (tel: 85-1111).
Camino Real (170 rooms) Punta del Sábalo (tel: 13-1111).
Caravelle Beach Club (118 rooms) Camarón Sábalo (tel: 13-0377).
Costa de Oro (382 rooms) Camarón Sábalo (tel: 13-5344).
De Cima (150 rooms) Av del Mar (tel: 82-7300).
El Cid (1,000 rooms) Camarón Sábalo (tel: 13-3333).
El Quijote Inn (67 rooms) Camarón Sábalo (tel: 14-1134).
Holiday Inn Sunspree (200 rooms) Camarón Sábalo 696 (tel: 13-2222).
Islas del Sol (75 rooms) Camarón Sábalo 696 (tel: 12-0088).
Los Sábalos (185 rooms) Loaiza 100 (tel: 83-5333).
Oceano Palace (200 rooms) Camarón Sábalo (tel: 13-0666).
Playa Mazatlán (425 rooms) Loaiza 202 (tel: 13-1120).
Puesta Del Sol (66 rooms) Camarón Sábalo (tel: 13-5522).
Riviera Mazatlán (225 rooms) Camarón Sábalo 51 (tel: 83-4611).
Solamar Inn (56 rooms) Blvd Sábalo 1942 (tel: 13-6666).
Torre Tropicana (169 rooms) Loaiza 27 (tel: 83-8000).
Vidafel (291 rooms) Sabal Cerritos s/n (88-0045).

Inexpensive
Caribe (21 rooms) Av del Mar 1020 (tel: 83-1955).
Club Playamar (57 rooms) Av del Mar 840 (tel: 82-0833).
Conquistador (60 rooms) Rafael Buelna 185 (tel: 83-2866).

Posada Don Pelayo (178 rooms) Av del Mar 1111 (tel: 83-1888).

Economy
Acuario (42 rooms) Av del Mar s/n (tel: 82-7558).

Restaurants
Specialising mainly in seafood and charcoal grilled steaks, and some have fancy names like **Senor Frog**, **El Shrimp Bucket** and **Sr Peppers** which serves choice lobsters and steaks cooked on a mesquite grill.

Nightlife
Caracol Tango Palace at El Cid is the leading night spot. There are many shows and discos; ask your hotel desk for a list.

HUATULCO

The Bays of Huatulco are located on Mexico's Southern Pacific Coast, in the state of Oaxaca. It is the government's biggest tourist project since Cancún.

Accommodation

Super Deluxe
Holiday Inn Crowne Plaza (135 rooms) Benito Juarez 8 (tel: 1-0044).
Sheraton (356 rooms) Benito Juarez s/n (tel: 1-0055).

Moderate
Castillo Huatulco (107 rooms) Santa Cruz s/n (tel: 7-0144).
Club Mediterranée (554 rooms) Bahia de Tangolunda (tel: 1-0033).
Posada Flamboyant (70 rooms) La Crucecita (tel: 7-0105).

BAJA CALIFORNIA

Baja California, 782 miles (1,260km) in length, and mainly desert, is longer than the peninsula of Italy, and attracts visitors because of its sea fishing and watersport, around its 2,111 miles (3,400km) of coastline. In some of the resorts there is a good development of hotels and prices are reasonable.

Sightseeing includes visits to the ruins of some of the early Spanish missions at **San Ignacio** and **Mulegé** and to caves where there are Indian paintings of hunting scenes, whose history is unknown and origins not yet completely understood.

Besides the main border towns of **Tijuana**, **Tecate** and **Mexicali** which are particularly popular with day visitors from the United States, there is a one hour

A statue of an Indian at Tijuana. The early Mesoamerican's main weapon was a club inset with obsidian blades that with one blow could cut off the head of a horse

The Cathedral at San José del Cabo

government has been encouraging the development of new resorts, such as **Loreto** and **San José del Cabo.**
Recently, the largest striped marlin was caught in these waters. At the extreme tip of the peninsula lies **Cabo San Lucas**, an idyllic spot where the waters of the Sea of Cortés and the Pacific meet. Golfers can play four world-class courses hereabouts – Cabo San Lucas, Cabo Real, Cabo del Sol and Palmilla.

further drive via a good toll road to the charming port of **Ensenada**, and about 22 miles (35km) from here, **La Bufadora**, a blow-hole that periodically spouts sea-water.
La Paz, made famous by John Steinbeck for its pearl divers, is popular for game fishing, which is so good off the coast of Baja California that the Mexican

WHAT TO SEE

PINTURAS RUPESTRES (CAVE PAINTINGS)
Carried out centuries prior to the arrival of Europeans, they bear hardly any resemblance to other Mexican art forms. Indian

legend relates that they are a product of a race of giants from the north. Difficult to reach, best departure points San Ignacio and Mulegé.

◆◆◆
SANTUARIO DE LA BALLENA GRIS (GRAY WHALE NATIONAL PARK)

Twenty miles (32km) from Guerrero Negro is where the visitor can see the sea mammals which have migrated from the icy waters of Alaska to Scammon's Lagoon to breed.

Accommodation

Loreto
Moderate
La Pinta Prado Inn (48 rooms) Madero s/n (tel: 5-0025).
Loreto Inn (235 rooms) Blvd Mision de Loreto (tel: 3-0700).

Inexpensive
Hotel Misíon de Loreto at Calle de la Playa 1 (tel: 3-0048), is situated east of the plaza, along the waterfront. The 33 rooms are comfortable, and some have good views of the Sea of Cortés. Also:
Oasis (35 rooms) Baja Calif s/n (tel: 5-0211).

Restaurants
The **Embarcadero** overlooks the beach and marina. Popular with local fishermen, its seafood dishes include fish tacos and grilled fish (tel: 5-0165).

Cabo San Lucas/San José del Cabo (now called Los Cabos)

Super Deluxe
The **Hacienda** in Cabo San

Lucas (tel: 3-0122) resembles an old Spanish hacienda with fountains and tropical gardens.
Finisterra (220 rooms) Domicillo Conocido (tel: 3-3029).
Presidente Inter-Continental (246 rooms) Blvd Mijares s/n (tel: 2-0211).
Westin Regina Los Cabos (243 rooms) Carr Transpeninsular Km 22.5 (tel: 2-9002).
Others include:
Cabo San Lucas (101 rooms) Rancho el Tule (tel: 3-0123).
Palmilla (71 rooms) Corredor Turistica a Cabo San Lucas (tel: 3-0582).
Playa las Glorias (187 rooms) Blvd Marina s/n (tel: 3-1220).
Solmar (90 rooms) Av Solmar 1 (tel: 3-3535).
Twin Dolphin (50 rooms) Carr Transpeninsular Km 11 (tel: 3-0256).

Moderate
Aguamarina (100 rooms) San José del Cabo Av Malecón 6 (tel: 2-0077).
Calinda Beach Cabo (125 rooms) Carr Transpeninsular a La Paz Km 4.5 (tel: 3-0045).
Howard Johnson (172 rooms) Paseo Finisterra 1 (tel: 2-0999).

Restaurants
There are many good restaurants and nightlife entertainment. Prices tend to be a little high in Los Cabos. **El Rey Sol** serves great Mexican dishes and the shellfish is excellent, too. **Rio Grill** ia an attractive waterfront restaurant with live music and candlelit dinners of steak and lobster. Try **La Paloma** for Sunday brunch.

SOUTHERN MEXICO

South Mexico is used here to describe the states of Oaxaca, Chiapas, Tabasco and part of Veracruz, although the latter is more to the east of Mexico City. It is a fascinating region, mostly mountainous, with lush jungle forests in certain areas, and with a near tropical climate.

OAXACA

Some 300 miles (483km) southeast of Mexico City, Oaxaca is a delightful provincial city set in a temperate and fertile valley, and ringed by the inspiring range of the Sierra Madre del Sur. The city and environs are steeped in pre-Columbian and Colonial traditions, making it one of the most interesting and attractive regions in Mexico. Visitors can see the ancient city ruins of **Monte Albán**, **Yagul** and **Mitla**. This is the home of the Zapotec and Mixtec Indians, and the considerable Indian population of the region gives rise to interesting markets and shops, which sell a dazzling array of hand-embroidered clothes, rugs, jewellery, leather and silver at inexpensive prices. **San Bartolo Coyotepec** is famous for black pottery, **Teotitlán** for hand woven *serapes* and **Yaluga** for raw silk shawls. On the 'Night of the Radishes', 23 December, booths are set up in Oaxaca for the display and sale of sculpted radishes portraying amazing nativity scenes.
Between Monte Albán and Mitla is one of the largest living trees in the western hemisphere.

Opulent baroque style is the hallmark of Santo Domingo, Oaxaca

Streets of houses in Oaxaca remain unchanged since the Colonial period, which, along with the churches of **Santo Domingo de Guzmán**, the **Basílica Menor de la Soledad**, the **Cathedral** and **San Juan de Díos**, reflect a golden age of architecture. Architecturally, one of the most interesting hotels in the whole of Mexico is the **Hotel Presidente**, the renovated 16th-century convent of Santa Catalina. The church of **Santo Domingo**, dating from the 17th century, is one of Mexico's greatest treasures. Inside it is a riot of baroque ornamentation. Benito Juárez, Mexico's greatest statesman, came from this region.

SOUTHERN MEXICO – OAXACA

WHAT TO SEE

CASA Y MUSEO BENITO JUÁREZ (HOUSE AND MUSEUM OF BENITO JUÁREZ)

Calle García Vigil 609

To understand further the influence and contribution which the Mesoamerican people have and continue to make to Mexico and her history, visit the home of her most famous president, Benito Juárez, who was a full blooded Zapotec. His background, rising from poverty to the highest position in the land, is similar in many ways to Abraham Lincoln, of whom he was a contemporary. Some of the rooms appear as they did in the middle of the last century.

MITLA

Twenty-eight miles (45km) east of Oaxaca

Mitla contains some of the most precious remains in Mexico: the Hall of Columns – palaces whose walls are covered in highly artistic Grecian-style ornamentation, and the Columna de la Vida (Column of Life), which, when grasped, is claimed to tell you how long you have to live.

MONTE ALBÁN ✓

Nine miles (14.5km) from Oaxaca

These ruins of a religious Zapotec and Mixtec town are unique. Positioned on a mountain top, they cover 15 square miles, (39sq km) and include the main square, the ball-court, an observatory, numerous tombs which honeycomb the hilltop and carvings referred to as 'dancers' (believed to be records of medical conditions and deformities).

MUSEO DEL ESTADO (STATE MUSEUM)

The museum is next to Santo Domingo Church and houses an incomparable collection of Zapotec and Mixtec gold, silver, jade and turquoise *objects d'art* and some of the most interesting relics found in a Mixtec tomb in Monte Albán. The workmanship is exquisite.

MUSEO RUFINO TAMAYO

Ave Morelos 503

A colonial mansion housing a pre-Hispanic art collection of pottery and sculpture originally belonging to the artist Rufino Tamayo.

YAGUL

About 21 miles (33km) from Oaxaca

The ruined Zapotec fortress city of Yagul is on top of a mountain and overlooks three levels of palaces, temples and the largest ball-court in the Oaxaca Valley. There is an excellent view of the valley from the top.

Accommodation

Super Deluxe

Camino Real (91 rooms) 5 de Mayo 300 (tel: 6-0611).

Hotel Presidente (see restaurant section).

Victoria (152 rooms) Lomas del Fortin 1 (tel: 5-2633).

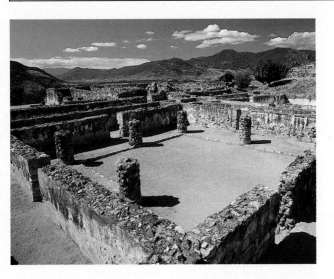

The Palace of Six Patios on the large archaeological site at Yagul

Moderate
Fiesta Inn (120 rooms) Av Universidad 140 (tel: 6-1122).
Fortin Plaza (93 rooms) Av Venus 118 (tel: 5-7777).
Misíon de los Angeles (175 rooms) Calzada Porfirio Díaz (tel: 5-1500).
San Felipe Oaxaca (160 rooms) Jalisco 15 (tel: 3-5050).

Inexpensive
Marqués del Valle (tel: 6-3677) is situated right on the plaza at Portal de Claveria. Some of its 95 pleasant rooms have splendid views over the square.
Best Western Hacienda La Noria (54 rooms) Av Hidalgo 918 (tel: 4-7844).
Calesa Real (77 rooms) García Vigil No 306 (tel: 6-5544).
Margarita (70 rooms) Calz Madero 1254 (tel: 6-6869).

Mesón del Angel (62 rooms) Javier Mina No 518 (tel: 6-6666).
Monte Albán (18 rooms) Alameda de León (tel: 6-2777).
Señorial (127 rooms) Portal de Flores (tel: 6-3933).

Restaurants
One of Oaxaca's specialities is *mole Oaxaque*, a spicy, chocolate-based sauce used on pork and chicken. Try **El Asador Vasco** (tel: 6-9719). As well as good food, entertainment is laid on nightly. Try **Nuu-Luu**, an attractive open-air restaurant. Here the food is varied and very reasonably priced.
Early evening entertainment can be enjoyed around the Zócalo. The **Hotel Presidente** has an excellent restaurant, **El Refectorio**. This 16th-century convent is now one of the most beautiful and unusual hotels in Mexico; don't miss seeing it (tel: 6-0611).

Tuxtla Gutiérrez

This is the capital of Chiapas and home of the *Marimba* bands which often provide evening entertainment at the hotels. The **zoo** on the south side of Tuxtla is well worth a visit. Placed on a hill, some of the walks are steep. **Cañon del Sumidero**, a magnificent gorge cut by the River Grijalva, lies 14 miles (22km) north of Tuxtla Gutierrez. It is one of the most spectacular natural sights, being 9 miles (15km) long and with walls that descend nearly 4,000 feet (1,200m). An entire tribe of Chiapa Indians threw themselves to death from here rather than face being slaves to the Spaniards. Boat trips are available from **Chiapa de Corzo**, a small town 12 miles (20km) east of Tuxtla, with a 16th-century Moorish-style fountain and museum of regional handicrafts.

Accommodation

Moderate
Bonampak Tuxtla (105 rooms) Blvd Belisario Dominguez No 180 (tel: 3-2050).
Flamboyant (118 rooms) Blvd Belisario Dominguez s/n (tel: 5-0888).
Real de Tuxtla (97 rooms) Carretera Pan-Am (tel: 4-1663).

Restaurants
Well worth a visit is **Las Pichanchas**, east of the Zócalo (tel: 2-5351) where you can get outstanding Mexican food, *marimba* music and weekly folkloric dances.

SOUTHERN MÉXICO

SAN CRISTÓBAL DE LAS CASAS

Seven thousand feet (2,134 metres) up in the Chiapas highlands, San Cristóbal is populated mainly by poor and exploited, but very dignified Chamula and Zinacantecas Indians, usually dressed in colourful traditional costume. The name of the city honours Bartolomé de las Casas, the first Bishop of Chiapas. Take warm clothing and an umbrella along, for it can be cold and wet in this area. San Cristóbal is the home of some of the finest Colonial architecture. Just north of the Zócalo lies the baroque church of **Santo Domingo** which is distinguished by its lovely pink façades. The former convent next door is the **Craftwares**

Museum, and local artefacts can be bought here.

WHAT TO SEE

◆◆
CASA NA BOLOM
Chiapa de Corzo
Former home of the Danish anthropologist, Frans Blom (lived in now by his widow), now a museum of local archaeology and ethnography, concentrating on the Lacandón Indians, the most remote and elusive of all Mexican tribes.

◆◆◆
LAGUNAS DE MONTEBELLO
A series of lakes, 88 miles (141km) southeast of San Cristobal, each with a different colour caused by minerals reflected in their waters, ranging from emerald green to turquoise.

Accommodation
Moderate
Di Monica (86 rooms) 5 de Febrero 18 (tel: 8-1363).
Flamboyant Español (54 rooms) Calle 1° de Marzo 15 (tel: 8-0726).

Inexpensive
El Molino de la Alborado at Apartado Postal 50 (tel: 8-0935), is close to the airport, and there is a 9-hole golf course.
Other include:
Bonampak (50 rooms) Calzada México (tel: 8-1621).
Palacio de Moctezuma (42 rooms) Av Benito Juárez No 16 (tel: 8-0352).
Parador Méxicanos (25 rooms) Cinco de Mayo (tel: 8-1515).
Rincón del Arco (21 rooms) Ejercito Nacional (tel: 8-1313).
Santa Clara (42 rooms) on the Zócalo (tel: 8-1140).

Restaurants
San Cristóbal has a range of small restaurants to suit most tastes. Dinner is taken early and there is not an active nightlife. With the present unrest, seek local advice on where to eat out.

VILLAHERMOSA

Villahermosa, capital of the state of Tabasco, is an important industrial centre for the oil industry. There is a good selection of hotels in the area.

WHAT TO SEE

◆◆◆
PARQUE LA VENTA (VENTA PARK)
This park, set on the outskirts of the city, is an outdoor Olmec museum displaying altars and massive carved stone heads, a curious puzzle with their flattened, negroid features, in a setting like the one in which they were originally found. Deer, monkeys and anteaters wander freely while alligator and jaguars can also be seen. There is also boating on the **Laguna de Ilusiones** (Lagoon of Illusions).

Accommodation

Moderate
Cencalli (120 rooms) Paseo Juárez (tel: 15-1966).
Choco's (72 rooms) Constitucíon (tel: 12-9044).
Holiday Inn (191 rooms) Paseo Tabasco (tel: 16-4400).
Howard Johnson (84 rooms) Aldama 404 (tel: 14-4645).
Hyatt Regency (210 rooms) Juárez No 106 (tel: 13-4433).
Maya Tabasco (160 rooms) Ruiz Cortines (tel: 12-1111).

Inexpensive
Don Carlos (116 rooms) Francisco Madero 418 (tel: 12-2499).
Miraflores (68 rooms) Reforma 304 (tel: 12-0022).
Plaza Independencia (90 rooms) Independencia 123 (tel: 12-1299).
Varesta (25 rooms) Prol Paseo Usumacinta 147 (tel: 13-6739).

Restaurants
The choice of food in Villahermosa reflects a Mayan influence. Next door to the CICOM Museum of Anthropology is **Los Tulipanes**, a spacious restaurant with a splendid river view. For a good paella try **Restaurant Reyna**.

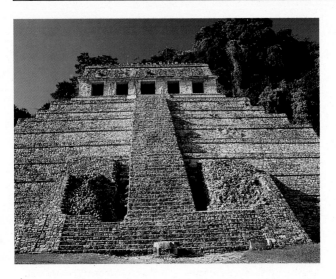

The Tomb of Inscriptions at Palenque is concealed in a nine-tier pyramid

◆◆◆
PALENQUE ✓

Although in Chiapas, this site is most easily reached by road from Villahermosa around 90 miles (145km) away to the northwest. In the jungle setting of Palenque lies a whole city, believed to have been the ceremonial centre of the great Mayan dynasty, which includes the **Templo de las Inscripciones** (Temple of Inscriptions) where the famous 'Man in the Jade Mask' tomb was found in 1946. Today, the visitor can climb the great stairway from the ground to the temple and then descend nearly as far down again to the burial chamber itself. Near by is the **Palace** complex and the **Templo de la Cruz Foliada (Temple of the Leafed Cross)** on a tiered pyramid. Its chamber, which was a sanctuary, has at the far end an altar covered by three linked panels of the cross. The cross, a stylised maize plant, was the symbol of life.

The cooling waters of the **Cascada Motiepa**, a waterfall, are just down the road from the site's parking area.

There is a selection of hotels. To the southeast of Palenque, located deep in the jungle of Chiapas is **Bonampak**. Here you will find some of the finest Maya murals discovered so far. The site can be reached by charter plane from either Villahermosa or San Cristóbal.

VERACRUZ AND ENVIRONS

Veracruz was for centuries Mexico's major sea port. From the docks, visitors can see the fortress of **San Juan de Ulúa**, built in 1582 to protect the port from pirates; later it became a notorious prison. In the heyday of Hollywood, many black and white films were made here. Veracruz is the home of the Latin American dance called the *bamba*. *Marimba* music remains a feature of evening entertainment around open air cafés.

Villa del Mar is the principal beach in Veracruz. Six miles (9.6km) out of the port, at **Mocambo**, is another fine beach bordered with pinewoods, and in a fishing village just beyond, called **Biza del Río** are good open air seafood restaurants overlooking the river.

Beaches on the **Isla Sacrificíos** are reached by a launch trip. Excursions take the visitor to **Jalapa**, where there is a fine anthropological museum, to the Totanac ruins at **Zempoala**, and to **Tlacotalpan** where the wealthy hid from pirates.

WHAT TO SEE

EL TAJÍN
The only major archaeological zone in the upper Gulf Coast region. Noteworthy ruins are the famous **Pyramid of the Niches** built by the Totanacs, the **Palace of Columns** and the great number of ball-courts.

EL VOLADOR
A religious rite, sometimes referred to as the *Flying Indians*, takes place every Sunday in **Papantla**. This thrilling feat involves four Indians leaping off a tall pole to which they are tied, and spinning to the ground, while a fifth plays a pipe while perched on the top (see page 15).

ACUARIO DE VERACRUZ
State-of-the-art aquarium, and a marine research centre.

Accommodation

Moderate
The **Emporio** (tel: 32-2222) with 200 rooms, overlooks the harbour at Paseo del Malécon. There are 3 pools, a roof garden and disco.
Hostal de Cortés (100 rooms) Blvd de las Casas (tel: 32-0065).
Howard Johnson (110 rooms) Avila Camacho (tel: 31-0011).

Inexpensive
The **Colonial** (tel: 32-0193) is situated right on the Zócalo at Miguel Lerdo 117. It is a well-maintained hotel with 215 rooms.
Others include:
Acuarío (90 rooms) Valencia (tel: 37-4422).
Real del Mar (51 rooms) Avila Camacho No 2707 (tel: 37-3634).

Restaurants and Nightlife
Seafood from the Gulf is the speciality in local restaurants. Buskers provide great nightly entertainment at the Zócalo. For discos and piano bars head for the hotels. The **Emporio** hotel restaurant and **Tilingo Charlie's** bar are popular with the locals. Dance clubs come and go and the most recent is the **Ocean** on Calle Ruiz.

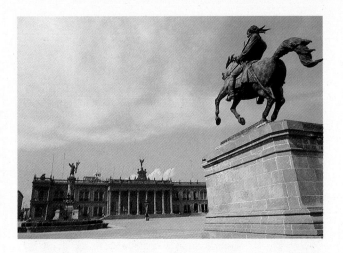

The statue of Benito Juárez outside the Palacio Gobierno, Monterrey

NORTHERN MEXICO

Reaching from the Sea of
Cortés, or Gulf of California, to
the Gulf of Mexico, Northern
Mexico is perhaps more of a
business area than a holiday and
resort region. With the
exception of the coastal strips,
the northwestern territory is for
the most part plains, mountains
and desert. The mountain
ranges are rich in minerals. In
other less harsh and difficult
domains than the desert lie the
grainfields with the coastal
fringes being particularly rich
farming country.
In northeastern Mexico is
Monterrey, the industrial capital
and third largest city with over
two million inhabitants. Within
this region a business traveller
with limited time off would have
a choice of visiting the largest
cities, some of considerable

architectural interest, of the five
states in this area which include
Coahuila, **Nuevo León**,
Tamaulipas, **San Luis Potosí**
and **Zacatecas**. For example,
the latter, which derives its
name from the Aztec words
zacatil (grass) and *tlan* (place), is
surrounded by the impressive
mountains of Mexico's Sierra
Madre Occidental, and
successfully combines the
roughness of its geographical
terrain with the aristocratic
flavour and elaborate
architectural and colonial design
of the buildings around the
zócalo, thus symbolising the
wealth that Zacatecas achieved
in the 18th century, as one of the
world's great silver mining
centres. Torreon, in Coahuila,
became a successful centre
for collectivised agriculture
after the Revolution.
From a more tourist point of

The **Fuente de la Vida,** *or Fountain of Life, is one of several in Monterrey's huge Gran Plaza*

view there is one trip that is a great experience; it is on the **Ferrocarril de Chihuahua al Pacífico,** (Chihuahua Pacific Railway) 'the world's most scenic railroad' between **Chihuahua** and **Los Mochis**. Here the **Barranca del Cobre** (Copper Canyon) route cuts through a rugged section of northern Mexico's Sierra Madre. Four times larger and 280 feet (85m) deeper than the Grand Canyon, the train takes 12 hours one way, covering some 400 miles (640km) and passing through 86 tunnels and over 39 bridges, providing breathtaking views of spectacular mountain scenery. the line's highest point is **Los Ojitos** at 8,681 feet (2,646m). There are two major, de luxe, air-conditioned trains departing every morning, at 07.00hrs from both Los Mochis and Chihuahua, at opposite ends of the line. Reserved tickets can

be purchased from both stations. To get the full benefit of the grandeur and beauty of the canyons, it is best to take the Los Mochis to Chihuahua route in order not to risk missing any of the magnificent scenery, as at certain times of the year it gets dark early.

Better still is to stay overnight en route at certain places such as **El Fuerte**, **Cuitéco**, **Cerocahui**, **Divisadero** and **Creel**. In some places, for instance Barranca del Divisadero, it is possible to ride on horseback along the edge of the canyons as well as to walk. At Creel you can visit the **Sierra Tarahumara**, home of the Tarahumara Indians, Mexico's most primitive and isolated tribe. Minibuses or jeeps are available to take you through the area.

THE YUCATÁN PENINSULA

The Yucatán Peninsula is the home of the Maya, one of the greatest civilisations ever known. It is studded with partly excavated archaeological sites. Many of these lie within a day's drive of **Campeche**, a fortified port rich in colonial architecture. Visitors can stay at some sites. Enquire at the Ramada Hotel in Campeche for more information. The region also encompasses the modern holiday playground of **Cancún**, on the edge of the Caribbean, which attracts a million visitors a year seeking sea, sand and sunshine.

MÉRIDA

Capital of the state of Yucatán and near the southern Caribbean coast, this colonial city, or 'White City' as it is known, was built in 1542, and straddles the site of the ancient ceremonial centre of Tiho, which was the last of the Maya strongholds to be defeated by the Spaniards. The Montejo family, who settled here afterwards, have a house, **Casa de Montejo**, dominated by a façade of bas-reliefs in the main square showing the arrogance of the Spanish knights standing on the heads of vanquished Maya. It is now a branch of the Banco Nacional de México. On the opposite side is the **Ayuntamiento City Hall**, with its beautiful doorways and murals depicting the history of Yucatán. Other buildings in this very attractive Zócalo are the **Cathedral** and **Palacio de Gobierno**, now the headquarters of the State government. Before the advent of synthetic fibres, this city was rich from the export of sisal. Now, with its whitewashed walls, squares with fountains, flower-bedecked parks and relaxed way of life, it provides an ambience of faded gentility, which is very soothing. It remains one of the main departure points, along with Cancún, to the important Maya sites of **Uxmal**, **Chichén Itzá** and **Tulum**, and is a scheduled stop on most of the organised tours of this part of Mexico. Hotels cover the range, some being in attractive neo-classical style, some of an older vintage.

WHAT TO SEE

◆◆◆ CHICHÉN ITZÁ ✓

75 miles (121km) east of Mérida
One of the biggest Maya archaeological sites in existence, it extends over six square miles (15.5 sq km). The huge ball-court, the size of a football pitch is the largest that has been found. The **Temple of Kukulkan** (Quetzalcoatl) is the centrepiece and is the result of a Maya-Toltec fusion. At the equinoxes, triangles of light and shadow fall on the ramp to give the appearance of the great serpent descending from the top of the temple (Heaven) to Earth. Note the **Temple of Warriors** with its snake-like columns and its Chacmol, a splendid reclining figure holding a vessel on which offerings to the gods were placed.

◆◆
COBÁ
30 miles (48km) inland from Tulum

Recognised as probably the biggest Maya site yet discovered and comparable in importance to Chichén Itzá, Cobá has a network of limestone-constructed, ceremonial roads, running over its 18 square miles (47sq km). It has been totally reclaimed from the jungle and work began in the early 1970s to excavate it. The task will probably take half a century to complete properly.

◆◆◆
TULUM
70 miles (113km) south of Cancún

When the Spanish first saw this city in 1518 they remarked that it was as large as Seville. It is one of the few walled sites, with a pyramid called 'The Castle'. The attraction really is its setting, perched on the top of a high cliff overlooking the Caribbean.

◆◆◆
UXMAL ✓

50 miles (80.5km) south of Mérida

A magnificent ruined Maya city with some of the finest proportioned and lavishly decorated buildings in Mesoamerica. Note in particular the oval **Pyramid of the Magician** in front of the beautifully laid out quadrangle of the **Nunnery**. After dark there is a spectacular sound and light show.

Accommodation (Mérida)

Super Deluxe
Hyatt Regency (300 rooms) Av Colon esq, Calle 60 (tel: 42-0202).

Legend says Uxmal's Pyramid of the Magician was made in one night!

Uxmal depended on rainfall for its water supply hence the Nunnery friezes devoted to the rain god Chac

Moderate
Casa del Balam (54 rooms) Calle 60 (tel: 24-8844).
El Castellano (170 rooms) Calle 57 (tel: 23-0100).
Holiday Inn (210 rooms) Colon 498 y Calle 60 (tel: 25-6877).
María del Carmen (70 rooms) Calle 63 (tel: 23-9133).
Mérida Misión (148 rooms) Calle 60 No 487 (tel: 26-9667).
Montejo Palace (90 rooms) Paseo de Montejo 483C (tel: 24-7644).

Inexpensive
The **Caribe** (tel: 21-9232), once a convent, is now a small hacienda-style hotel on Calle 59, close to the Zócalo. Its 60 rooms are clean and comfortable and there is a small roof-top pool and a deck which overlooks the plaza.
Others include:
Alfonso García (80 rooms) Calle 86B No 587 (tel: 24-9366).
Aluxes (109 rooms) Calle 60 (tel: 24-2199).
Cayre (100 rooms) Calle 70 (tel: 21-1652).
Colón (54 rooms) Calle 62 No 483 (tel: 23-4355).
Colonial (73 rooms) Calle 62 No 476 (tel: 23-6444).
Del Gobernador (61 rooms) Calle 59 No 535 (tel: 23-7133).
Del Parque (20 rooms) Calle 60 No 495 (tel: 24-7844).
Gran (36 rooms) Calle 60 No 496 (tel: 24-7730).
Paseo de Montejo (92 rooms) Paseo de Montejo 482 (tel: 23-9033).
Peninsular (49 rooms) Calle 58 No 519 (tel: 23-6902).
Posada Toledo (20 rooms) Calle 58 No 487 (tel: 23-2256).

San Luís (18 rooms) Calle 61 No 534 (tel: 21-7580).
Sevilla (45 rooms) Calle 62 No 511 (tel: 21-5258).

Economy
El Caminante (32 rooms) Calle 64 No 539 (tel: 23-6730).
Mucuy (24 rooms) Calle 57 No 481 (tel: 28-5193).

Staying on Site
Chichén Itzá and Uxmal archaeological sites are outstanding. Some people will want to stay overnight to have more time to see them. Hotels at Chichén Itzá include **Mayaland** (tel: 6-2777) and **Mision** (tel: 6-2671); at Uxmal is **Mision Park Inn** (tel: 24-7308).

Restaurants
Mérida's specialities include meat and fish baked in banana leaves and a delicious *sopa de lima* (chicken in lime broth). For crystal chandeliers, balcony tables and menus to suit all palates, try **La Belle Epoca** (tel: 28-1928). **Amaro** (tel: 28-2451) is a good choice for vegetarians.

CANCÚN

Cancún has developed in the last two decades from a tiny fishing village of 115 people and a stretch of empty beach to a world-class playground with a year-round population of 70,000. Great credit is due to the Mexican government, who foresaw the holiday potential in this area and encouraged development for tourism. This Costa Brava of the Caribbean attracts visitors from all over the world, offering a resort holiday to suit all tastes and budgets. Cancún is actually an island – a thin stretch of sand connected to the mainland by two bridges. The city beach of **Playa Tortugas** is the centre of activities. It is also another departure point for tours to many interesting Maya sites. Cancún is also a port of call for cruise ships and a busy shopping centre. Besides visiting **Cozumel**, from here many visitors also take the ferries out from nearby **Puerto Juárez** or **Punta Sam** to the attractive little **Isla Mujeres**, where the Spaniards first set foot in what is present-day Mexico.

Accommodation
Supermarkets can provide for those who want to self-cater and hotels abound in every price range. Cancún and its environs has over fifty hotels and below are listed those in the hotel zone on the Kalkulkan Boulevard.

Super Deluxe
Camino Real (381 rooms) (tel: 83-0100).
Hyatt Caribe (198 rooms) (tel: 83-0044).
Hyatt Regency (300 rooms) (tel: 83-0966).
Krystal (325 rooms) (tel: 83-1133).
Sheraton (622 rooms) (tel: 83-1988).

Moderate
The **Casa Maya** (tel: 3-0555) is only three miles (5km) from the city. Its 350 rooms are large. Amenities include three pools, tennis courts, moped rental and a restaurant. Popular with

Cancún abounds with luxury hotels like the Hyatt Regency seen here

families but a little expensive. Others include:

Aristos (268 rooms) (tel: 83-0011).

Beach Palace (146 rooms) (tel: 83-1177).

Calinda Beach (470 rooms) (tel: 83-1600).

Club Lagoon (90 rooms) (tel: 83-0811).

Flamingo Resort (90 rooms) (tel: 83-1544).

Miramar Misión (225 rooms) (tel: 83-1755).

Playa Blanca (161 rooms) (tel: 83-0071).

Inexpensive
Cancun Clipper (140 rooms) (tel: 83-1366).

Nightlife
Discos are as numerous as pebbles on a beach. Every night of the week there is a Mexican fiesta at one of the big hotels and for something different, try an evening 'pirate cruise' over to Isla Mujeres, or a lobster dinner cruise.

Restaurants
In Cancún there are over 1,000 restaurants and seafood is a speciality. **El Pescador** (tel: 84-2673) provides good seafood at moderate prices. For an expensive dinner try **Bogart's** (tel: 83-1133), arranged in Casablanca style of the 1940s, or **El Mexicano** for a folkloric dinner show (tel: 83-2220). There is dancing till midnight after the show.

COZUMEL

The island of Cozumel is easily reached from the mainland by ferry, being just over a dozen miles (19km) offshore. It can be reached by hydrofoil or aircraft from Cancún, or by ferry from **Playa del Carmen** and **Puerto Morelos**. Cortés regrouped his fleet from Cuba here, before sailing to Veracruz to start his conquest of Mexico. The island is 30 miles (48km) long and nine miles (14.5km) wide and is a port of call for cruise ships. Duty-free shops line the waterfront of its main town, **San Miguel**. Visitors come from all over the Americas to scuba dive and snorkel – the **Chankanaah Lagoon**, south of Cozumel is the best spot. **Palancar**, off the southwest coast, is the second longest coral reef in the world, after Australia's Great Barrier Reef. It is now a national park.

Accommodation

Moderate
La Ceiba (tel: 2-0844) is south of San Miguel on Paradise Point. It is a favourite place for scuba divers and has a beach which offers fine snorkelling. Other amenities on offer are tennis, a sauna, good restaurant, cocktail lounge and boat rentals can be made.
Others include:
Cabañas del Caribe (bungalows, 56 on the beach) North Zone (tel: 2-0072).
Cantarell (100 rooms) North Zone (tel: 2-0144).
Club Cozumel Caribe (236 rooms) Playa San Juan Km 4.5 (tel: 2-0100).

El Cozumelaño (100 rooms) Playa Santa Pilar (tel: 2-0050).
Fiesta Americana (164 rooms) Carr a Chankanaab Km 7.5 (tel: 2-2686).
Melia Mayan Plaza (180 rooms) Carr Santa Pilar Km 6 (tel: 2-0411).
Plaza las Glorias (163 rooms) Av Rafael Melgar Km 1.5 (tel: 2-2000).
Presidente Inter-Continental (253 rooms) Carr a Chankanaab Km 6.5 (tel: 2-0322).
Sol Caribe (321 rooms) Playa Paraiso Km 2.5 (tel: 2-0700).

Inexpensive
La Perla (24 rooms) Carr a Chankanaab (tel: 2-0188).
Maya Cozumel (48 rooms) Calle 5 Sur No 4 (tel: 2-0011).
Méson San Miguel (97 rooms) Av Juárez (tel: 2-0233).
Paraiso Caribe (37 rooms) 15a Av Nte 594 (tel: 2-0740).
Villablanca (20 rooms) Carr Costera Km 5 (tel: 2-0730).
Vista del Mar Av Melgar (tel: 2-0545).

Restaurants and Nightlife
People dine early in Cozumel and most of the restaurants are in the town. Enjoy Maya Night on Monday and Fiesta Mexicana on Thursday at the **Melia Mayan** hotel (tel: 2-0411), and Caribbean Party Night at **Hotel El Cozumelaño**. For perfectly prepared seafood dishes, the relatively expensive **Arrecife** restaurant at the Hotel Presidente (tel: 2-0322) leads the way. Family-run **La Choza** is known for its lobster and red snapper at reasonable prices (tel: 2-0958). **El Moro** (tel: 2-3029) is also family-run.

PEACE AND QUIET

Wildlife and Countryside in Mexico

by Paul Sterry

Geographically speaking, Mexico is an extremely varied country, even by Central American standards. It is dominated by a central mountainous plateau, which is flanked on either side by peaks, some of which rise to over 12,000 feet (3,600m). Volcanoes are frequent features, and the seismic activity of the Earth's crust also manifests itself in the occasional earthquake.

To the east of the mountains, the land drops steeply to the coastal fringes of the Caribbean and Gulf of Mexico, while to the west lies the Pacific Ocean. These coastal lowlands are markedly different in both vegetation and wildlife from the higher

The River Grijalva cuts through the impressive Cañon del Sumidero

elevations inland. The Baja California and Yucatán peninsulas are also of interest; their comparative isolation has ensured many unique features.

Mexico City and the Central Highlands

With an expanding population, which some recent estimates claim to be fast approaching 15 million, Mexico City and the surrounding districts are unlikely destinations for the holiday naturalist. It is certainly true that, with the exception of a few hardy and tolerant species of bird, little wildlife interest remains within the boundaries of the metropolis. However, by making day excursions away from the hustle and bustle and choking air pollution, visitors can still find plenty to see

PEACE AND QUIET

around forested archaeological ruins and in national parks. Crime is a real threat to Mexico City's visitors, particularly those with such luxury items as cameras and binoculars. Exercise common sense when using these items, and try to make any excursions with a few like-minded companions.

Close to the centre of Mexico City lies Chapultepec Park, one of the largest and most popular urban recreational areas. Visitors from Europe may be somewhat intrigued to see introduced house sparrows flourishing alongside native birds such as Inca dove, house finch, canyon wren and American robin. Travel west towards Toluca along Highway 15 and you begin to ascend the hills and mountains which finally limit the city's expansion.

By turning south off Highway 15 at La Venta you can reach the Desierto de los Leones National Park, an extensive area of comparatively unspoilt fir forest. Although it is some way from the city, solitary exploration is still not to be recommended, but visitors should still manage to see birds such as red warbler, Mexican chickadees, pygmy nuthatch and gray silky-flycatcher. Similar areas of forest can be found in the Valle de Bravo, 100 miles (160km) west of Mexico City, the Lagunas de Zempoala National Park, south of the city near Cuernavaca, and on the slopes of Volcan Itzaccíhuatl, east of Mexico City. To the northeast of Mexico City lies the famous pre-Columbian city of Teotihuacán, dominated by the Pyramids of the Sun and the Moon. The surrounding desert landscape is dotted with cottonwoods and agave cacti, and harbours lizards and birds such as vermilion flycatchers, turkey vultures, canyon wrens and curve-billed thrashers.

Northern Central Mexico

Northern Central Mexico is the Mexico of the movies. This upland plateau is a land of arid plains, deserts and mountains which stretch from the USA border south as far as San Luís Potosí and Guadalajara. Modern agriculture may have changed the face of parts of the landscape, with arable fields replacing the natural thorn scrub, but vast areas of desert still remain. In addition, there are pockets of marshland and pools as well as forest-clad

Cacti

More than any other country in Central or South America, Mexico is a land of cacti. Indeed, few serious cactus enthusiasts fail to tour the country at least once in their lifetimes. Several larger species, such as the prickly pear, have been exported to other parts of world, but America is their native home with the northern, central highlands holding perhaps the greatest diversity of all Mexico's regions. Cacti come in all shapes and sizes from small, compact cushions to the giant 'organ pipes' of the saguaro. What they all have in common is an ability to store water in times of drought, an essential quality considering Mexico's arid climate.

mountain slopes to add to the diversity of the wildlife and scenery.

Deserts are usually defined as regions where less than 6 inches (150mm) of rain falls each year, a criterion which much of Mexico more than meets.

Associated with cactus vegetation is an extraordinary range of desert animals, each adapted in its own way to the rigours of the environment. Some use the cacti in a variety of unusual ways: woodpecker's excavate nest holes which later may be taken over by elf owls, and roadrunners nest among the dense spines for protection. Many of the desert creatures

A cardon cactus forest flourishes in Baja California's arid climate

are active only at night, hiding in burrows or under boulders during the heat of the day. Rattlesnakes are well-known desert residents, but there are also lizards, ranging from tiny species to the large gila monster, and feeding on insects such as beetles.

Scorpions also come out at night to feed on insects and other small prey.

After dark, desert rodents such as kangaroo rats are sometimes seen in car headlights and many are taken by predators such as coyotes and great horned owls. Most of the desert's other birds are diurnal and frequently encountered species include curve-billed thrashers, cactus wrens, brown towhees, turkey vultures, American kestrels, Inca doves and mourning doves.

PEACE AND QUIET

Yucatán

The Yucatán peninsula harbours a surprising range of habitats, some of which are rather uncharacteristic of Mexico as a whole. Although bordered to the southwest by a belt of tropical rainforest, much of Yucatán is far too dry for this habitat. Dry tropical forest gradually disappears towards the end of the peninsula, where arid thorn and cactus scrub predominate. Yucatán is justly famous for its Mayan ruins, but for the naturalist it is the coasts which are the highlight. Sandy beaches, rocky outcrops, coral reefs and mangrove-lined estuaries support a host of birds, mammals and reptiles. The ruins of Chichén Itzá and Uxmal are the best preserved and most accessible of Yucatán's Mayan remains.

Both are surrounded by tropical forests, which are full of wildlife and well worth exploring.

A fork-tailed flycatcher

Iguanas, social flycatchers, ruddy ground-doves and groove-billed anis might all be seen in the ruins, while ocelots, coatimundis, spider monkeys, armadillos and iguanas and forest birds such as plain chachalacas, Yucatán jays, turquoise-browed motmots and masked tityras can be found in the surrounding jungle.

Mérida, the capital city of Yucatán state, is a good base from which to explore the northern coast. The channels of the Río Lagartos and the nearby saltworks lure thousands of greater flamingos, as well as several species of herons and egrets, plus brown pelicans, magnificent frigatebirds, laughing gulls and numerous migrant waders. Alligators and manatees, although scarce, still occur.

The Ría Celestún National Wildlife Refuge, to the west of Mérida, is an excellent destination and can be explored by boat. Flamingos spend the winter here and great egrets, snowy egrets, green backed herons, roseate spoonbills, neotropic cormorants, belted kingfishers, turkey vultures and numerous waders can be found all year. On the east coast of Yucatán, Isla Cozumel, Isla Mujeres and Isla Contoy are worth a visit for the marine life, birds and archaeological remains.

Palenque, Chiapas

Palenque, in the southeastern state of Chiapas, is one of the most famous and best preserved archaeological sites in Mexico. Dominated by its famous pyramid, in Mayan times Palenque was an important city set in the heart of the jungle. Today it is still surrounded by tropical rainforests, and this fascinating habitat provides both a wonderful contrast to the ruins and superb opportunities for wildlife enthusiasts.

Rainforests, particularly areas as extensive as at Palenque, are an unusual sight in Mexico. This is partly due to man's influence and partly because most of the country's climate is too dry to support this habitat. However, in this region of Chiapas, visitors can find steamy jungles with trees laden with bromeliads, orchids and other epiphytes, vines and creepers as well as beautiful waterfalls and species of birds and mammals not found in other regions of Mexico.

The forests are full of insects: cicadas call from high in the trees and butterflies fly along glades and paths.

Around the ruins themselves and the forest edge, birdwatching is somewhat easier than in the jungle itself. Black vultures, roadside hawks and black hawk-eagles occasionally soar overhead, while boat-tailed grackles, groove-billed anis, rufous-tailed hummingbirds, great kiskadees, brown jays and clay-coloured thrushes can be found.

Within the forest, observing wildlife can be rather frustrating at first. The high, dense leaf canopy, low light levels and shy nature of some of the birds and mammals can prove a challenge. Before long, however, visitors learn to follow sounds and movements and the

Countless butterflies are found in the forest around Palenque

creatures reveal themselves. Armadillos and coatimundis feed on the forest floor and share this habitat with little tinamous and ruddy quail-doves, and howler monkeys scream from the treetops. Hummingbirds with delightful names such as purple-crowned fairy and white-bellied emerald often come to investigate intruders, but such exotically-named birds as violaceous trogons, keel-billed toucans, blue honeycreepers, rufous pihas and lovely cotingas do not invite attention.

Catemaco

Catemaco lies about 105 miles (170km) southeast of Veracruz along Highway 180 close to San Andrés Tuxtla. The town is on the western shores of Lago Catemaco and wetland wildlife can easily be seen. Catemaco also lies within easy reach of a

PEACE AND QUIET

wide variety of other habitats, and this helps boost the range of species that can be encountered. There are patches of lush tropical rainforest plus beaches and estuaries on the nearby Gulf.

Lake Catemaco is an immense body of water which can be explored both from its margins and by boat. Rich fish populations support large numbers of birds: neotropic cormorants, pied-billed grebes and least grebes frequent the open water, while snowy egrets, cattle egrets, little blue herons and great blue herons stalk along the shores. Several species of kingfisher also occur and these include belted, ringed, Amazon and pygmy kingfishers.

Open farmland and roadside verges are good for squirrel cuckoos, groove-billed anis, rufous-tailed humming birds, great kiskadees, social flycatchers, brown jays, clay-coloured thrushes and Montezuma oropendalas. This latter species nests in colonies, weaving large, flask-shaped nests suspended from the branches of trees.

As you travel further away from the town, patches of rainforest appear. The road which leads to the Estacion Los Tuxtlas Veracruz, north of Sontecompan, is a particularly good area, and trees festooned with epiphytic plants, vines and creepers can be seen.

This is a public road, but the research reserve belongs to the Instituto de Biologia, Universidad Nacional Autónoma de México. Birds such as

Great blue herons are among the many birds living on Lake Catemaco

masked tityras, red-legged honeycreepers, blue-gray tanagers and hummingbirds such as violet sabrewings, fork-tailed emeralds and long-tailed hermits can be expected.

The shores of the Gulf of Mexico make a contrast to the rainforests. Some of the beaches are good for shells, and the estuaries and mangroves harbour spotted sandpipers, grey plovers, semi-palmated plovers, laughing gulls, royal terns and magnificent frigatebirds.

Although there is much of interest throughout the year, birdlife is most diverse from October to March when migrants from North America visit the region.

Villahermosa

Villahermosa is a bustling city in the state of Tabasco in southeast Mexico. Parks and gardens within the boundaries of the city contain a surprising number of birds, but it is the surrounding countryside which offers the best opportunities for the birdwatcher. Cattle ranching has created large areas of open land and, together with the natural marshes and wetlands of the region, the open country birds can be seen extremely well. By driving the back roads to the south and east of Villahermosa, visitors will soon find fields, ditches or wetland areas full of wildlife. Almost anywhere is likely to be good, but for the best birdwatching opportunities be sure to visit the Usumacinta Marshes, a huge area of wetland to the east of the road to Frontera, and the wetlands to the south of the city around Jalapa.

Along the roadsides, double-striped thick-knees feed unobtrusively in the fields and bright green lizards sunbathe on tree trunks. Birds such as scissor-tailed flycatchers, fork-tailed flycatchers, great kiskadees, boat-tailed grackles and groove-billed anis can be seen perched on fence posts or in branches.

The area is particularly good for birds of prey, and species such as laughing falcons, roadside hawks, black vultures, turkey vultures, yellow-headed vultures, Aplomado falcons and white-tailed hawks are quite regularly seen.

One of the more unusual raptors of Usumacinta is the snail kite, which feeds almost exclusively on the large, amphibious apple snails found in the marshes. The kite's specially adapted hooked beak enables it to extract the snail's body from its shell. Piles of the broken remains can be found beneath favourite feeding perches.

The wetlands host a wide range of species which are widespread throughout Central America. Typical birds include neotropic cormorants, which perch in groups to dry their feathers, anhingas, white and brown pelicans, roseate spoonbills, wood storks, great egrets, snowy egrets and limpkins and black-bellied tree-ducks. Jacanas delicately pick their way across the marsh vegetation on incredibly long toes, and lucky visitors may even see a beautifully marked pinnated bittern or ringed kingfisher perched on a branch overhanging the water. This latter species is the largest of its kind in the Americas and is the size of a crow.

Green lizards are seen frequently

PEACE AND QUIET

Mexico's Atlantic Coast

Mexico's eastern coast faces on to the Gulf of Mexico, which is contiguous with the Atlantic Ocean. The land is varied both in appearance and vegetation, being influenced by the climate, the altitude and by man. On the coastal plain, open grassland areas cleared for cattle ranching and agriculture contrast with dense forests, while on the coast itself sandy beaches, mangroves and lagoons can be found. Inland, the lowlands soon give way to hills and mountains, which provide both relief from the heat and contrasting wildlife. Many beaches are good for shells, although their distribution on the sand is often curiously localised. In common with most popular coastal areas of the world these days, beaches near to resorts are generally scoured regularly, so you may have to travel farther afield for the best results. Beaches and mudflats on Mexico's Atlantic coast are also good for birdwatchers: willets, egrets, magnificent frigatebirds, brown pelicans and royal terns are regularly seen. Brown pelicans catch fish by plunge-diving into the sea for fish while the frigatebirds attack other seabirds, forcing them to disgorge their last meal.

The shallow, coastal waters are rich feeding and breeding grounds for fish and all sorts of other marine animals. A whole new world is revealed with the use of snorkel and mask. Colourful starfishes, sea urchins, sea fans, manta rays, parrotfish and bass are among the delights that await the visitor.

The proximity of the ocean moderates extremes in temperature and the summer rainfall encourages the growth of dense forest. The rainfall becomes heavier, and its effect more profound, the further south along the coast you travel, and in some areas the jungles resemble true tropical rainforests. In this terrain, armadillos and tinamous forage among the fallen leaves, and motmots, hummingbirds, trogons and woodpeckers haunt the higher canopy.

Further inland, as you move up the slopes of the Sierra Madre, pockets of cloud forest still remain. Here the trees appear stunted, seemingly weighed down by astonishing growths of creepers and epiphytic orchids and bromeliads.

Mexico's Pacific Coasts

The Pacific coast runs from the Arizona border south to Guatemala and harbours some of the country's major holiday destinations. For the visitor with an interest in natural history, the region offers the best of both worlds, a wonderful climate and beautiful beaches, and coastal lagoons, mangroves and lush jungles. Holiday visitors to coastal resorts need not necessarily restrict themselves to lowland habitats; the foothills of the Sierra Madre shadow the coast for much of its length and offer widely differing wildlife. Even close to holiday centres such as Acapulco, San Blas and Mazatlán, beaches are the haunts of coastal birds such as laughing gulls, brown pelicans, magnificent frigatebirds, royal terns and willets. Unless deliberately molested, these species often show remarkable indifference to the presence of man and give good opportunities for observation.

Shell Collecting

Shells are the abandoned homes of marine molluscs which thrive in the waters off Mexico's coast. They are often cast up on the shores and would be much more of a feature of many sandy beaches were it not for avid collectors. If you want to find such treasures as keyhole limpets, cowries, moon shells and murex shells you will have to travel away from the popular resorts. Be careful to check each shell for hermit crabs before you collect them and never buy shells from shops: invariably this has involved the needless death of the shell's original owner. Those shells lying loose on the beach will have died naturally.

Coastal lagoons act as magnets for water birds. Even those which are close to the resorts can be good: Laguna Coyuca and Laguna Papagayo near Acapulco are considered especially rewarding.

Abundant populations of amphibians and fish encourage birds such as kingfishers, cormorants and several species of herons and egrets. Waders (called shorebirds in North America) are transient migrant visitors, but ever present are the black vultures.

Mangroves and coastal jungles are always worth exploring, both birdlife and for invertebrate inhabitants. For a change in habitat and temperature too, drive inland into the hills of the Sierra Madre, where forests of oak and pine can be found.

Baja California

Baja California is the finger-like projection which runs down the west coast of Mexico. It is the longest peninsula in the world, bordered on the west by the Pacific Ocean and to the east by the Gulf of California. Baja is one of the least known areas of Mexico, best explored either from Tijuana in the north or from

Cormorants on Usumacinta Marshes

PEACE AND QUIET

La Paz in the south. It is, however, one of the richest destinations for the naturalist: whales, seabirds and abundant marine life are found around the coast, while inland, cactus-rich deserts give way to mountains, some cloaked in dense forests. Baja California is a region of sparse rainfall. Conditions become more arid the further south you travel, this trend being more noticeable on the eastern side of the peninsula, where prevailing winds from the west have already shed what little moisture they contained. Mountain slopes in the north of Baja are often cloaked in woodland comprising a mixture of pine and oak. Birds found here are reminiscent of California, with species such as acorn woodpecker, white-breasted nuthatch, western bluebird, violet-green swallow and plain titmouse often being seen. At higher elevations, pine trees predominate and here pygmy nuthatches, mountain chickadees and Clark's nutcrackers may be found. Around the coast, the mangroves and saltmarshes which visit the estuaries on the west of Baja are breeding grounds for marine life such as crabs and fish, as well as egrets, herons, ibises and spoonbills. Away from the shores, however, the vegetation is typically adapted to the arid conditions. Low thorn scrub is dotted with desert plants such as elephant trees, ocotillos and lomby, as well as nearly 100 species of cacti. These range in size from miniature cushions to the straggling sour pitaya and

immense, 70-foot (21m) pillars of the cardon cactus.

The Baja deserts are also home to a wide variety of animals. Many of the creatures are active by night and scorpions, lizards and rattlesnakes often seek cover during the day. Coyotes, too, are more often seen and heard at dusk and black-tailed jackrabbits and racoons also favour this time of day. The birdlife can, however, be seen by day, and cactus wrens, Anna's hummingbirds, roadrunners, burrowing owls, pyrrhuloxias, California quails and gray thrashers all occur.

Gray Whales

One of Mexico's greatest wildlife spectacles is undoubtedly that of California gray whales, which visit the coastal lagoons of Baja California each winter to mate and give birth to their young. Once hunted to the verge of extinction, the world population of these immense leviathans is now beginning to recover. A recent estimate put the figure at around 17,000 and a large number of these are breeding adults which visit Mexico each year. Baja California is the only place in the world where the gray whales come to breed, and the opportunities to view them are unsurpassed.

The whales spend the summer months feeding in the rich Arctic waters off Alaska. Because their newly born calves cannot withstand the cold temperatures in the far north, the adult whales migrate south each autumn to the warmer waters of Baja California. The whales arrive in

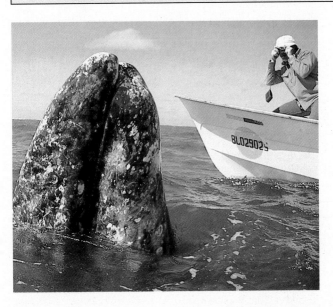

Visitors are able to view the gray whales at very close quarters!

December, give birth in January and February and begin the return trip in March accompanied by their young. This is also the time when the next generation is conceived. The main destinations for the gray whales are three lagoons on the west coast of Baja: Scammon's Lagoon, Laguna San Ignacio and Bahía Magdalena. Here the estuarine waters are shallow, warm and protected from the full force of the Pacific by chains of barrier islands. Magdalena Bay, the southernmost of the breeding grounds, is the most accessible, and can easily be reached by car from La Paz. Boats are available in San Carlos and whales can even be seen from the shores. Alternatively, several specialised whale-watching tours such as Biological Journeys, California (tel: 707-839-0178) operate trips from Sandiago or from San Carlos. Because of the enclosed nature of all three lagoons, the whales can be seen at extremely close range. Fortunately for visitors, they are gentle creatures and often appear curious about the human intruders into their environment. They will sometimes raise their heads out of the water and stare at visitors. These close encounters also allow the huge barnacles which encrust their skins to be examined in some detail. More dramatic still are the breaching displays which are occasionally seen – the whale lunges out of the water and crashes back on the surface.

PEACE AND QUIET

Mar de Cortés (Sea of Cortés)

Sometimes known as the Gulf of California, the Sea of Cortés is one of the richest marine areas in the world. Since the days when John Steinbeck was captivated by it, the area had lost little of its charm until the last decade or so. Fish and other marine creatures still flourish and, in turn, support thriving populations of seabirds, dolphins and whales. However, over-exploitation of the sea's resources is having a noticeable effect upon stocks and the long-term prospects for the region need to be addressed by the Mexican government with some urgency.

There are more than 50 islands here, each with its own unique character. The coral reefs and beaches which fringe them are home to starfish, sand dollars, manta rays and sharks. Cacti are abundant on almost all of the islands and some have large mammals such as black jackrabbits and coyotes. Some harbour colonies of sealions and seabirds such as blue-footed and brown boobies, ospreys and pelicans.

The region is especially famous for its whales. These are not the gray whales of western Baja, but finbacks, humpbacks, sei and killer whales. Blue whales are also regularly encountered. Despite their size, they are extremely wary of boats. It is thought possible that older individuals may even remember the days of whaling and associate boats with death. Reputable and experienced boat captains are, however, usually able to get extremely good views of these magnificent creatures.

Los Islotes in the Sea of Cortés,

FOOD AND DRINK

Food

The most common mis-conception about Mexican food is that it is mostly composed of chillies and is so hot that it will blow the top off your head! It is true that the chilli figures prominently but there are 200 varieties of chilli, ranging from mild to the very hot. In fact, there is only really one exceptionally hot chilli which is used in the Yucatán and was popular among the Maya. This is the *habanero*, which the Mayans called 'the crying tongue'. Maize, or 'Indian Corn' or Sweetcorn is probably the most widely used ingredient in Mexican cooking followed by the chilli and then the tomato and avocado.

Part of the fascination of Mexican cooking is that it has drawn its influences from so many and varied sources over hundreds of years and represents a wide combination of Indian, European and American tastes. To the Aztecs we are indebted for chocolate, vanilla, potatoes, maize, pumpkins, squash marrows and mangoes as well as a cornucopia of other fruits, nuts and seeds.

The Spanish conquistadores brought beef and dairy products to Mexico as well as chickens, goats, pork, wheat, oils, sugar, olives, garlic, and a knowledge of viticulture as well as the vines themselves. They also introduced apples, oranges, pears, peaches and melons. Hence, it is not surprising that the cuisine of Mexico is highly developed and that different parts of this huge country have also developed their own style. In Baja California, seafood figures prominently, especially in delicious seafood soups. Lobster, abalone (an edible mollusc with an ear-shaped shell) crabmeat, turtle steak and quail are served all along the Pacific Coast. Here, haddock, clams, oysters, lobster and palm hearts, stuffed snapper fish, shrimp often cooked in a batter of beer, charcoal-grilled seafood and suckling pig are popular and readily available. Another favourite dish is *ceviche*, uncooked seafood marinated in natural lime juice.

In the northern states of Mexico, local favourites include steak, spare ribs and kid grilled over a fire of mesquite, and beef, lamb and bacon skewered together, usually served on a bed of rice. In Guadalajara the visitor will find a dish of shredded beef or chicken mixed with tomatoes and onions and grilled, a popular choice.

The kitchen of the Convent of Santa Rosa in Puebla, now the Museo de Artesanías is the place where the sauce known as *mole poblano* evolved. I say evolved rather than created as no one chef could have suddenly decided to concoct a sauce of over 60 ingredients including chocolate, chillies, ground nuts, various fruits and some 30 spices. Turkey served in this sauce is now considered a national dish and, incidentally, the sauce has a very subtle flavour, not at all sweet. It can also be served with chicken and *enchiladas*.

FOOD AND DRINK

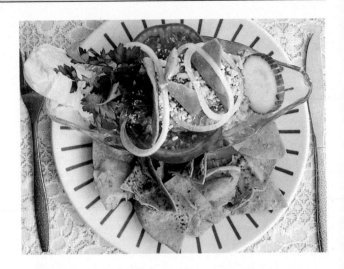

Guacamole *made with avocados, served with tacos, small corn pancakes*

In Oaxaca you will find *mole* offered with *tamales.* Oaxaca's *mole* is much darker in colour and milder in taste than that of Puebla. *Tamales* are generally made from steamed corn husk or banana leaf. The *tamales* are usually filled with meat, vegetables, or chilli beans. Some are quite solid and are eaten like bread and the large ones have excellent filling qualities for hungry travellers. In Chiapas, they make a delicious cheese, shaped like a cannon-ball. It is eaten plain or with a spicy meat filling. Yucatán is recognised for its fragrant and delicately flavoured dishes. The juice of sour Seville oranges mixed with garlic and black pepper is used for seasoning. Specialities include *tortilla* dipped in pumpkin seed sauce and filled with crumpled hard-boiled egg,

suckling pig wrapped in a banana leaf and baked slowly, baby shark and Moro crab. The great variety of coconut dishes and the famous almond cake are popular with the visitor. Lime soup and the liberal use of lime juice helps to combat bacteria and can help to avoid upset tummies frequently referred to by Americans as 'Moctezuma's Revenge'.
In Veracruz, the red snapper fish, *huacinango*, is famous and so is the *plato jarocho*.
Although the ubiquitous Tex-Mex food abounds throughout the country it will be clear by now that there is more to be enjoyed in the way of Mexican food.
Meals at the Mexican restaurants mentioned compare favourably in price with similar European or American establishments but not if the

visitor orders imported wine, spirits or liquors, all of which are heavily taxed.

Drink

In the last ten years Mexican wine has improved in quality and is worth trying. The names to look out for are *Domecq*, *Santo Tomas* and *Hidalgo*. Mexican beer is very good and goes down well with the Mexican dishes. *Negra Modelo*, *Léon Negra* and *Nochebuena* are popular brands. The powerful *tequila*, distilled from the maguey cactus is the best-known Mexican spirit – it can be drunk straight with salt and lemon or mixed into a cocktail. The country's best mineral water comes from Hacienda Spa Penafiel.

Mexico has an excellent variety of non-alcoholic drinks and the exceptional quantity and quality of fruit available in Mexico, gives rise to a huge range of delicious drinks.

These are easy on the pocket and quite likely to wean adults and children away from the ubiquitous manufactured beverages. *Horchata*, a sweet melon-seed drink is traditional. Many fruit juice bars are found throughout the country.

If you don't like sugar in your coffee you must be specific about this. As a general rule coffee (*café*) is drunk sweet, and many restaurants buy their coffee with the sugar already added (*café de olla*). Instant coffee is readily available, and the decision regarding sugar can be your own. Indian or China tea (*té*) is not readily available, but it is worth trying

té de manzanilla (camomile tea), and *yerba buena* (mint tea). Incidentally, coconut milk tastes delicious and is an excellent antidote if you are suffering from 'holiday tummy'.

Glossary

Mexican dishes you are most likely to come across:

ate: a jellied paste usually made from guava or quince.

cabrito: boiled goat – mainly found in northern Mexico.

cajeta: usually made from goat's milk which is caramelised.

carnitas: chunks of pork, deep fried.

ceviche: a seafood cocktail of uncooked, marinated seafood with chopped onion, tomato, pepper, oil and avocado.

chilaquiles: fried *tortilla* chips with sauce and cheese.

chillies rellenos: peppers stuffed with cheese and minced meat, fried in batter and served in hot tomato sauce.

chongos: curdled milk, mixed with egg, syrup and cinnamon.

chorrizo: spicy sausage.

cochinita pibil: a Yucatán speciality – suckling pig cooked in banana leaves.

enchilada: this is a fried, flat cake of corn meal (*tortilla*) containing various fillings such as meat, fish, cheese.

guacamole: pulped avocado flesh mixed with onions, tomatoes, chillies and yoghurt. Used as a dip with *tacos* or as a side salad.

mixiote: mutton cooked in the skin of maguey spikes, in corn husks or banana leaves and served with a spice sauce.

picadillo: filling of minced meat, mixed with tomato and onion with various seasonings.

pozole: a very highly seasoned soup, including hominy (maize) kernels, chick peas, pork, radishes, sausage, tomato and whatever else the cook has to hand!

quesadilla: various ingredients fried inside *tortilla* dough, such as cheese and strips of chilli, meat or mashed potato squash flower.

taco: a taco is a *tortilla* (see below) wrapped around various ingredients and then fried.

tamales: steamed corn dough stuffed with pork or chicken and chilli sauces, wrapped in a dry corn husk or a banana leaf. They can also have a sweet filling.

torta: a sandwich made with French bread. It will be filled with either ham, chicken, cheese, beans or pork and will almost certainly contain some chillies.

tortilla: the versatile and ubiquitous *tortilla* is the staff of life in Mexico. It has many variations but in its basic form it is a thin cake of corn meal (wheat meal is used in the north). It is served with meals, spread with sauces and rolled up to hold various fillings.

SHOPPING

Unless you are very strong minded indeed you must prepare to be carried away by the shopping possibilities of Mexico, either in the *tianguis* (native market) or the boutiques in the many resorts. The visitor will find that there are two kinds of market. The permanent markets attract people from towns and villages round about and take place on one or two days each week. The markets of Oaxaca, Guadalajara and Acapulco are among the best. The temporary markets are found in small towns and rural areas and on the outskirts of large cities and even major crossroads. They are particularly lively and worth visiting during the holiday seasons around Christmas and Easter and on the special fiesta days.

Arts and Crafts

As with its cuisine, Mexico, with its arts and crafts, has many indigenous traditions and has also developed and made its own many external influences and traditions. Ceramic ware of every kind abounds throughout the country. It was well established when the Spaniards arrived. Until that time, the pottery was single fired at a low temperature in open fires and this pottery can still be found and is the least expensive. Single-fired, unglazed pottery is not safe to use for cooking or food because the pottery contains lead salts which will activate with certain foods and become poisonous.

The Spaniards introduced the potter's wheel, the enclosed kiln and lead glazes to Mexico. High firing kiln temperatures now make ceramics more durable. Majolica is the finest and consequently the most expensive pottery. The skill of making it was introduced into Puebla in the 16th century. The authentic majolica is decorated with Arab heraldic motifs of shields, lions and eagles. However, the potters of the Metepec, inspired by the straightforward candlestick introduced by the Spaniards, developed this into what is known as the Tree of Life design, adorned with birds and flowers (sometimes standing ten feet high). There is also (although not for the faint-hearted) the Tree of Death, which takes the form of a skeleton with branches decorated with skulls.

In the state of Michoacán, especially near Pátzcuaro, the visitor will find attractive dishes in 'earth' colours of browns and greens. In San Bartolo Coyotepec, near Oaxaca, families produce interesting black pottery. Distinctive red glassware is found in Guadalajara, especially in Tlaquepue where the glass blowing can also be seen, and crystal in Monterrey.

Weaving is the second most important craft in Mexico, and Oaxaca is the area renowned for the production of magnificent woollen blankets and rugs. The natural dyes are more expensive than commercial ones but far more beautiful. In Teotitlán del Valle rugs are woven to your own specifications. In Michoacán blankets and rugs are of simple design and soft natural colours but with a looser weave. Fine serapes, a fashion 'item' in Europe are also available in Saltillo. The *rebozo*, which can be either a shawl or stole, is made of wool or in some cases, silk. Very fine ones will pass through a finger ring and San

Luís Potosí is especially famous for them. In Tlaxcala, the cheerful striped Saltillo spread is woven.

The Huichol Indians make yarn paintings which are constructed on a base of plywood and covered with beeswax. Then they press acrylic yarn into the base to form a picture, usually on a mythological theme. The pictures were originally made as offerings for the gods.

Yucatán is famous for its hammocks, and Mérida has the widest selection. You can choose from a variety of materials, ranging from twine, which is the cheapest, to luxuriously comfortable linen.

There is a wide variety of traditional clothing, much of it elaborately embroidered with designs from different regions. The Oaxaca wedding dress is one of the most attractive and popular.

Tijuana is the place to buy all kinds of leather goods. The further south you go the more you will pay. Leather goods are also available in Léon (famous for boots and shoes), Guadalajara, Jalisco and Guanajuato, Oaxaca and Chiapas.

Mexico is the world's largest producer of silver and the Mexicans are very skilled in working it and other metals into lovely jewellery. Some of the best jewellery and other silver items are found in Taxco, Guadalajara and Mexico City. In Oaxaca you will find exquisite reproductions of pre-Columbian jewellery in gold and silver, as well as fine gold filigree work. Michoacán is famous for its copperware, best found in Pátzcuaro market and government craft stores. Bark paper paintings are sold throughout the country and you will find the greatest variety and best quality comes from the state of Guerrero.

Collectors of religious art are well served, with many artists creating *retablos* (primitive religious paintings on tin) and *milagros* (miracles) which are tiny religious amulets made of silver shaped like hearts or limbs and *santos* (wooden carvings of saints).

In Uruapán, the craftsmen are renowned for their lacquered chests, boxes and furniture made of hardwood. *Equipales* furniture, traditionally made of pigskin and wood, is found in the state of Jalisco.

Mexicans also make beautiful toys. They are charming and imaginative, reflecting the Mexican's love of children. Toys include puppets, snakes hiding in matchboxes, tops and rag dolls.

Fonart is the name of a chain of government shops throughout the country which offer a wide variety of typical art and craft products at set prices. You don't have to haggle here but their prices may be slightly higher than average although the quality will be good. A visit will give you an idea of what is potentially available elsewhere. Bargaining is accepted in most places and is common in the markets, so drive a hard bargain if you like. In remoter places where Indians offer home-made wares, remember most live below the poverty line.

ACCOMMODATION

Mexico offers a wide range of accommodation from ultra modern and elegant hotels to more modest establishments known as *casas de huespedes* (guesthouses). Room prices in all Mexican hotels are controlled by the Secretaría de Turismo (Ministry of Tourism) and there is a five-star rating system, similar to that in Europe, with a wide price range between one and five star.

When booking you should bear in mind that most accommodation rates are just that – they do not include meals. The cheaper hotels rarely provide a private bathroom but in only slightly more expensive ones there may be the option to pay an additional sum for this. Specific accommodation has been listed by Area. In categorising the hotels, the editor has simplified the classification. *Super Deluxe* refers to *Gran turismo* hotels where prices are usually very expensive. *Moderate* refers to price in terms of European equivalents and not to the category of hotel which is mainly 5- and 4-star. *Inexpensive* includes 3- star and 2-star hotels, and *Economy* refers to 1-star hotels.

There are also hostels but these are often run-down and away from the centre of the town and frequently no cheaper than local hotels. Apartments and villas are useful to families who want to be self-catering for economic reasons. Many condominiums, including luxury properties, are available with cooking facilities.

These brightly-coloured parrots found in Acapulco are typically Mexican

Helpful Hint

December is the high season.
Hotel rates are considerably
lower during the rest of the
year, and at times when the
hotels are not full it is possible to
negotiate on price.

There is a variety of chain hotels
throughout the country. Many
international hotel chains are
represented and where they
are, accommodation may be
booked through their offices
abroad. These are the major
hotel groups with hotels in
Mexico:

Aston Hotels and Resorts, Best
Western International, Holiday
Inns International, Hyatt, Inter-
Continental, Marriot, Princess
Hotels International, Quality Inns
International (known as Calinda
Hotels in Mexico), Kamada,
Sheraton, Utell/Stouffer
Presidente, Villa Vera, and
Westin.

Some have special facilities
which include golf courses,
tennis courts and marinas.

NIGHTLIFE AND ENTERTAINMENT

Mexico City has a rich cultural
life and its own world-famous
dance troupe, the **Ballet
Folklórico** which performs
regularly on Wednesdays
(21.00hrs) and Sundays (09.30
and 21.00hrs) at the **Palacio de
Bellas Artes** (National Institute
of Fine Arts) on Plaza Central
Alameda. Here you can also
attend operas and concerts. The
National Auditorium, in
Chapultepec Park, is a less
expensive venue, and concerts
are also held at two halls near
the Perisur shopping centre:
Ollin Yoliztli and
Nezahuacóyotl. Near Bellas
Artes is **El Teatro de la Ciudad
de México** (Theatre of the City
of Mexico).

Tickets for the theatre, cinema,
sports and bull fights in Mexico
City can be bought, with a
10 per cent surcharge, at the
Boletrónico electronic service;

but they must be bought at least 24 hours before the performance or event. Hotel desks have up-to-date information on the whereabouts of the service.

Mexico's smaller towns will not usually provide a very lively nightlife, and visitors may find hotels their best bet for late-night entertainment and dancing. However, the major towns and cities have plenty of action; see the individual regions described earlier in the book for selected listings of discos and other nightlife.

WEATHER

Hollywood films have left the impression on many minds that Mexico is a hot arid land filled with desert, where only the cactus and a few hardy bandits can survive the climate. The temperature and rainfall depends mainly on altitude. Unlike people living in northern Europe, Mexicans do not have to go south for their sunshine, they have to descend.

The hot regions of Mexico, *tierras caldas*, are those below 10,000 feet (3,000m), such as the coast, the Yucatán, and the Balsas Valley. Here the average temperature is over 25°C (80°F) and in the summer often over 38°C (100°F). Such regions are the home of birds of colourful plumage and supply most of the exotic Mexican fruit, which visitors love to eat. Temperate regions, *tierras templades*, exist between 3,000 and 5,000 feet (914m and 1500m) and here is grown the robust maize which is the staple diet of so many

CIUDAD DE MÉXICO

☂ June–September
mm ☼ February–May   °C

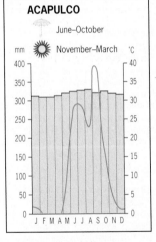

ACAPULCO

☂ June–October
mm ☼ November–March   °C

Mexicans. In this region the average temperature is between 15° and 21°C (60° and 70°F). Above this altitude lie the cold lands, *tierras frías*, or valleys enclosed by the cordilleras of the Sierra Madre Occidental and the Sierra Madre Oriental. In this region, with temperatures about 13°–18°C (55°–65°F), farmers grow wheat, maize and European species of fruits and vegetables. If visiting these areas it is advisable to have some warmer clothes as the daytime temperature can fall by 7.5°C (20°F) at night. However, not to totally disillusion keen film goers, it should be noted that Mexico does produce the greatest variety of cacti in the world. These grow in the arid deserts in the north of Mexico and the date palms of San Ignacio and Kada Kaurahang in Baja California match the finest groves in the Sahara. Incidentally, the name 'California' is derived from *calida fornax*, meaning 'hot oven'.

HOW TO BE A LOCAL

Mexico is a rich mix of races and cultures. Most of today's population is made up of *mestizos* – Spanish-Indians – but there are many 'pure' Indian communities. About 50 or so tribes form the core of the descendants of ancient Indian tribes, and many retain their old tribal lands, including communities such as the Tatrahumaras, Mayas and Yaquis, and the Tzotzils and Tzeltals in the Chiapas highlands. Most of those descended from central Mexican tribes now live in villages around the Valley of Mexico. About three to four million people are officially said to be 'full blood' Indians, still speaking their native languages and holding on to their traditions. Although many of the Indians have taken up

Christianity, not all have, and most combine the Christian tradition with their own religions and practises. Generally, visitors will find Mexicans friendly and polite but rather formal; you are not likely to blend in by being over-familiar. Sexual roles are still quite strictly defined in Mexico; among the *mestizos* particularly, *machismo* exerts a strong influence and men can display an aggressive, swaggering image, while assuming a fiercely protective attitude to the women of their families. The maternal role is vitally important and mother–son bonds can be especially strong. Foreign women, particularly from the West and travelling alone, should be prepared for the *macho* approach to women, which they may encounter in Mexico (see Personal Priorities below). The Indian population tends to display rather different characteristics, which can seem more passive. Although frequently very poor, 'pure' Indians have a most extraordinary dignity, which has perhaps been bequeathed to them from their ancient background. They, like other Mexicans, appreciate courtesy and respect from visitors. If you know something about Mexican history and politics and can discuss it you will make friends very quickly. And they appreciate it if you make some attempt to speak their language. But most of all they appreciate old world charm and courtesy. If you make close Mexican friends you will find they always give each other little gifts.

PERSONAL PRIORITIES

There are plenty of pharmacies in Mexico (see **Directory**), and the general run of toiletries can be obtained from all but the smallest communities. But it is as well to bring certain items with you; aspirin, medication for minor injuries, insect repellent, contact lens solution, film, tampons and contraceptives. If you have health problems and require special medicine, bring what you need and keep it in its original package to avoid drug suspicion.

Do not carry drugs, as heavy fines and jail sentences can be imposed. If anyone approaches you trying to sell drugs, tell them to go away immediately: it could be a police trap. Nudity is against the law; be careful even when bathing in remote areas. Homosexuality is not against the law except between adults and minors.

Women travelling alone may well receive unwelcome attention. The best way to respond to comments or harassment is to ignore them; they are more often a nuisance than a threat.

Women should not go into *cantinas*, which are all-male.

SPECIAL EVENTS

Fiestas

Mexico has so many fiestas every year that it is only possible to list those which are celebrated nationwide.

1 January – New Year's Day. In the provinces many agricultural and livestock fairs take place around this date.

6 January – Feast of the Epiphany or Día de los Reyes (Day of the Kings). Commemorates the bearing of gifts to the Infant Jesus. It is also the day that the 'Three Kings' bring gifts for Mexican children who set out their shoes hoping to have them filled.

17 January – Feast of Saint Anthony, The Blessing of the Animals. Household pets as well as cows, pigs and chickens are decked with flowers and ribbons and taken to church to be blessed.

2 February – Candlemas Day, or the Blessing of the Candles is the Feast of the Purification of the Virgin Mary. Impressive fiestas take place in Tlacotalpán and Veracruz.

5 February – Constitution Day. Celebrates the National Charter, which officially ended the Revolution of 1910.

February/March (date varies) in the week leading up to Lent which begins on Ash Wednesday – Mardi Gras festivities in the seaport cities.

March/April (date varies) Holy Week. Candlelit processions and Passion Plays.

April/May – Aquascalientes. Fería de San Marcos (San Marcos National Fair). Attractions include bullfights.

1 May – Labour Day. Parades, speeches. Everything closes.

3 May – Holy Cross Day. Celebrated by construction workers, who place crosses on top of unfinished buildings.

5 May – Anniversary of the Battle of Puebla (1862) in which Mexican troops defeated the Napoleonic invaders. Major celebrations nationwide.

10 May – Mother's Day. Special celebrations throughout Mexico.

15 May – San Isidro Day. Dedicated to the patron saint of farmers and agriculture.

1 June – Navy Day. Celebrated in major port cities with wreath-laying ceremonies.

May/June (60 days after Easter) Corpus Christi. Religious ceremonies, and in Mexico City, children dressed in native costume are taken to the cathedral in the Zócalo for a blessing. In Papantla, Veracruz, the famous 'flying birdmen' perform their breathtaking dance, *El Volador*.

24 June – St John the Baptist. Marked by religious services, processions and special fairs. In San Juan del Río, Querétaro the statue of the saint is taken to the river for its yearly bath.

16 July – Feast of Our Lady of Mount Carmel. Celebrated throughout Mexico with fireworks, games and bullfights. In San Angel, Mexico City there is a beautiful Flower Show.

25 July – Feast of Santiago (St James). Religious services and processions. Mexican-style rodeos are often held.

15 August – Feast of the Assumption of the Virgin Mary. Religious ceremonies and processions as well as the famous Bull Running in Huamantla.

1 September – State of the Union address given by the President. Banks and government offices close.

15–16 September – Independence Day. Starts on the night of 15th when, all over Mexico, public officials raise Hidalgo's call '*Grito de Dolores*'

that launched the War of Independence. In Mexico City, at 23.00hrs on 15th, the President of Mexico gives the shout from the balcony of the National Palace before a crowd of over half a million people gathered in the Zócalo. This is followed by a spectacular firework display. On 16th there is a military parade from the Zócalo to the Independence Monument.

4 October – Feast of St Francis of Assisi. Processions and parties. People called Francis or Frances receive gifts.

12 October – National day or Columbus Day (Día de la Raza). Called Day of the Race because Columbus' discovery marked the beginning of a new race made up of Hispanics and indigenous people.

1 November – All Saints Day. Religious ceremonies and processions.

2 November – All Souls Day (Día de la Muerta – The Day of the Dead). Candlelit all-night vigils are held at local cemeteries.

20 November – Anniversary of the Mexican Revolution of 1910. Parades throughout the country.

12 December – Feast of the Virgin of Guadalupe. The patron saint of Mexico is honoured.

16–25 December. The Christmas season features nightly *posadas* or processions with some people dressed as Joseph and Mary looking for room at an inn *(posada)*. Each night, the procession stops at a different house, asking to be let in to the building.

CHILDREN

A holiday in Mexico is great fun for children as there are so many marvellous beaches and special amusements for them. Mexico City, in particular, has an amusement park and zoo in **Chapultepec Park** and a marine park called **Atlantis**. Also in the park are several museums – Technology, Anthropology and Natural History. The **Ballet Folklórico** in the Palace of Fine Arts is particularly lively. Boat trips on the lagoons at the **Floating Gardens of Xochimilco** and the **Reino Aventura** (Adventure Park), **Zacango Zoo** and **Plaza Show**, with its prehistoric section and baby animals, are all within reach of Mexico City. Further afield are mining towns, caves and, of course pyramids and other ruins, as well as attractions like **Cici** marineland in Acapulco and amusement parks and zoos in Puebla, Monterrey, Guadalajara and Morelia. If you are travelling with children it is a good idea to take a selection of familiar medicines in a medical kit. Disposable nappies and ready prepared baby foods are available. Mexicans adore children and are very family-orientated.

There are big transport and hotel price reductions for children and in many hotels they get free accommodation if they sleep in the parents' room. Many restaurants have special cheaper dishes for children. Tummy upsets are common, so consider carefully what you offer your children. Don't buy ice cream on the beach and avoid home-made sweets. There are hundreds of miles/kilometres of sandy beaches but there is often a strong undertow just off the shore. Pay attention to the colour of the flag that is flying on the beach and if in doubt use the swimming pool.

TIGHT BUDGET

The low cost of transport and cheap accommodation available combined with the weakness of the peso against other strong currencies makes living on a tight budget fairly easy. However, the developed resorts, big cities and along the border, are more expensive. It is possible to eat cheaply in Mexico, but you may have to choose your establishment carefully. A snack bar or café is known as a *café, merendero, comedor* or *lonchería*. These cover a wide range of quality and cleanliness, though the food is never expensive. You can also eat in the market *fondas*, where the kitchen and the food are both on view and you can see what you are ordering. Bargaining is an accepted practice for shoppers – but should not be attempted in restaurants, government shops, hotel shops, or where the prices are fixed (*precios fijos*).

Buses are efficient as well as cheap, the same applies to Mexico City's metro system. Tolls on new highways are now as much as 40c a mile, making them prohibitively expensive. Likewise, internal domestic flights, which used to be cheap, have become expensive.

DIRECTORY

Arriving

Entry Formalities

Passports: Required by all except nationals of the USA and Canada holding proof of citizenship.

Tourist Card: Necessary for all visitors to Mexico. A Tourist Card ('FMT' in Spanish) is an entry–departure document (not a visa) which must be obtained before entry into Mexico. The card is issued free of charge by Mexican embassies (or consulates), tourist offices, travel agencies, or airlines serving Mexico. The areas of Mexico to be visited and the length of your stay (up to 90 days) must be specified. A Tourist Card is valid for **ONE** entry only, but is **NOT** required by American citizens who intend to spend no more than **three days** in Mexico, in border towns or ports.

Visas: A visa (replacing a Tourist Card) is required by nationals of Australia and New Zealand.

Under 18 years old

All persons under the age of 18 years if not travelling with **both** parents must contact the Mexican Embassy before departure.

By Air

Direct non-stop scheduled flights from London to Mexico City are only available from British Airways. They fly three times a week – Tuesday, Thursday and Saturday – from terminal 4 at Heathrow. Flights depart at midday and arrive into Mexico City at 16.30hrs local time. Return British Airways overnight flights also leave on Tuesday, Thursday and Saturday, departing 18.25hrs from Mexico City. Other scheduled airline routes to Mexico from London, with a stop *en route* in the US include American Airlines, Continental and Delta. Many airlines fly from London to North America to airports where it is possible to pick up another flight by a Mexican airline such as Aero México, Mexicana, Aero California and Taesa down into Mexico. For example, British Airways fly direct to Los

Angeles, and from there Aero California flies on to some 30 destinations throughout Mexico. Direct flights to Mexico from different destinations in Europe are available from Air France, Iberia, KLM and Lufthansa.

Air fares are in a constant state of flux, therefore if you have a tight budget it is worth shopping around for the best bargains. If speed and convenience are the chief priorities, then a direct British Airways flight is a natural choice. Travel agents are a useful source of information on these matters.

Out of Britain, there are now some 60 tour operators packaging holidays in Mexico. Among the leaders are such companies as American Fly Drive, Cox and Kings, Bales Tours, British Airways Holidays, Cathy Matos, Club Mediterranee, Cosmos, Hayes and Jarvis, Kuoni, Thomas Cook, Thomson Travel, Trailfinders and Twickers World, some of whom provide charter flights.

Mexico City (*Benito Juárez International*) is located 4½ miles (7km) east of the city (travel time 20 minutes). Buses to the

Benito Juárez airport, Mexico City

city leave every 15 minutes between 06.00–22.00hrs. The return is from the Camino Real Hotel, Reforma Street (same hours).

Courtesy coaches are laid on by some major hotels. The metro station, *Terminal Aérea* (Line 5) – **NOT** *Aeropuerto* – is a 5-minute walk from the airport terminal, however there is a limited luggage allowance on the metro. For a taxi, go to desks marked *Venta de Boletos*; they will sell you a ticket which you present to any waiting car marked *Transporte Terrestre*.

Acapulco (*Internacional General Juan M Alvarez*) is situated 16 miles (26km) east of the city (travel time 30 minutes). Public bus to the city every 10 minutes (05.00–24.00hrs) and some hotel courtesy coaches. Taxis can be expensive; shared Chevrolet *combis* provide a better deal.

Guadalajara (*Internacional Miguel Hidalgo*) lies 12 miles (20km) south of the city (travel time 30 minutes). Bus to the city every 10 minutes (05.00–24.00hrs) plus courtesy coaches operated by some larger hotels.

Monterrey (*General Maríano Escobero*) lies 15 miles (24km) northeast of the city (travel times 45 minutes), bus and taxi services available.

Departure. Upon departure from the country, passengers have to pay airport tax which is, at the time of going to press, US$10 or the equivalent amount in pesos.

By Bus

North American services operated by Greyhound and Trailways run regularly to all major border crossings, and at the larger of these, their buses take passengers on to Mexican bus stations. Both companies are able to reserve through-tickets with their Mexican counterparts. For services in Mexico see **Public Transport**.

By Rail
There is no direct rail connection between the USA and Mexico. You have to cross the border by some other form of transport or on foot, to connect up with Mexican rail services (see **Public Transport** section).

By Road
The main points of entry from the USA into Mexico are: Mexicali from San Diego; Nogales from Phoenix/Tucson; El Paso/Ciudad Juárez from Tucson and Alberquerque; Eagle Pass/Piedras Negras from Del Río, San Angelo and El Paso; Laredo/Nuevo Laredo from Houston, San Antonio and Del Río; Brownsville/Matamoros from Houston and Galveston. (See also **Driving**).

By Sea
A great number of cruise ships include Mexico in their itinerary. Many originate from across the Gulf at Miami and Fort Lauderdale, calling in at resorts such as Cancún and Cozumel in the Caribbean. Others originate from Los Angeles and San Diego and sail along the Pacific coastline calling in at Cabo San Lucas, Acapulco, Zihuatanejo, Ixtapa and Puerto Vallarta. Still others include both coasts and pass through the Panama Canal. Among the cruise lines which call in at Mexico are Cunard Line, Dolphin and Majestic Cruise Lines, Princess Cruises, Royal Caribbean Cruises, Royal Viking Line and Swan Hellenic.

Camping
Mexico has few organised campsites. Most trailer parks are just off major highways and not pleasant for pitching tents. You can camp in the national parks and no permits or fees are required. The best camping is in Baja or on the Pacific coast where there are pine forests and lakes.

Chemist (see **Pharmacist**)

Crime
Despite soaring crime rates there is no undue danger, provided you stick to the beaten-track. Even in Mexico City, the scene of most serious crime, there is little more threat than the average inner city, though, as in all cities, there are areas best to avoid. Drug offences are the most common cause of **serious** trouble. A jail sentence can be expected for foreign visitors in the possession of even small quantities of drugs. For most tourists, however, the biggest worry is petty theft and pick-pockets. Money should never be too conspicuous; when travelling keep an eye on luggage.

Currency
At the time of writing, there are no currency controls on tourists, but large amounts of currency must be declared, and any

amount of Mexican currency can be reconverted upon leaving. Be careful about being short changed (see **Money Matters**).

Customs Regulations

Visitors over the age of 18 years can bring into Mexico the following goods duty-free:
400 cigarettes
or 2 boxes of cigars
or up to 250 grams of tobacco; 3 litres of spirits or wine; a reasonable quantity of perfume or eau-de-cologne; other goods up to the value of US$300, or equivalent; one photo, movie or video camera and up to 12 rolls of unexposed film or video cassettes.

Disabled

Disabled travellers are likely to find that Mexico does not generally cater for their needs.

Driving

Bringing a car into Mexico requires motorists to be issued with a different kind of tourist card from other visitors (see **Arriving**) which ensures they cannot leave without their car. A Mexican car insurance policy, which is expensive, is also required – it is available from agencies on both sides of the border but probably more easily negotiated in the USA. Most foreign licences are valid in Mexico but European ones may be unfamiliar so it is a good idea to carry an International Driving Permit (available from the AA in Britain – it is different from the one which covers driving in the USA).

Many visitors from overseas like to fly and drive or hire a car while on holiday. This can be arranged as many of the international car-hire firms have offices at airports, city centres and in resorts. There are many local operations, too, but make very sure you are well insured against accidents. There are cars in Mexico that would never pass their roadworthy tests back home.

Breakdown

To help motorists, Mexico has an effective 'Green Angel' *(Angeles Verde)* service, a fleet of white and green, radio-dispatched emergency vehicles which patrol the roads and highways. Labour is provided free, although a tip is appreciated. Spare parts are charged at cost. If you need assistance and are not 'spotted' call the Green Angels on (5) 250-8221.

If you see an accident you should **not** go to help, but notify the first policeman or 'Green Angel' patrolman that you can find. If you move an injured person you can be accused of *mal medicinia* and if the person dies, you can even be accused of causing the death.

Parking

Parking is not easy in cities and if you wish to avoid being towed away, use an *estacionamiento* (parking lot).

Roads

Mexico's highway system is well-developed with tolls payable for use of motorways.

New motorways include Acapulco, Mexico City, Mazatlán, Nogales, Mérida, Cancún, Nuevo Laredo and Monterrey. Away from the large centres of population roads are quite often narrow, winding and pot-holed. Also look out for *topes* (sleeping policemen) across the road, before and after most villages.

Electricity
The supply is 110 volts AC, 60 Hz, though fluctuations in the current can occur. Sockets accept simple two (flat) pin plugs. Most North American electrical appliances can be used, but appliances from Britain, Australia or New Zealand will need a voltage transformer, unless fitted with a dual-voltage switch. A plug adaptor is also necessary.

Embassies and Consulates
The main embassies are all in Mexico City but several countries have consular representatives in other towns across the country.
Australia–Plaza Polanco Torre B, Jaime Balmes 11 (tel: (5) 395-9988).
Canada–Schiller 529 (tel: (5) 254-3288).
New Zealand–Homero 229 8th floor (tel: (5) 281-5486).
UK–Rio Usumacinta 30 (tel: (5) 596-633).
US–Av Paseo de la Reforma 305 (tel: (5) 221-0042).

Emergency Phone Numbers
Federal Police (*Highway Patrol*)   (5) 684-2142
Fire   (5) 768-3700
Green Angels (*Angeles Verde*) Tourist Patrol
          (5) 250-8221
Government Police   06
Mexico City Emergency Number   07
American British Cowdray Hospital   (5) 515-8359
Missing Persons   (5) 658-1111
Tourist abuse/complaints
          (5) 250-0493
(24-hour tourist hotline)   (5) 250-0123

Entertainment Information
Local tourist offices (*Turismo*) can give details of events that are going on in their area. The English-language newspaper, *Mexico City News* has a useful listings section. A weekly publication published on Friday called *Tiempo Libre* also gives information about current events.

Health Regulations
There are, at present, no inoculations required to enter Mexico, unless you have visited a cholera infected area within the two weeks prior to your entry to Mexico, in which case a cholera vaccination certificate is demanded. The greatest threat to health in Mexico is water – it should be boiled or sterilised. Milk should be boiled.
Some form of health insurance is essential when travelling to Mexico. Public health care can be fairly rudimentary but on the whole, the medical facilities in privately-run hospitals and clinics are quite good. Your hotel or embassy should be able to refer you to an English-speaking doctor or dentist if necessary.

Holidays

The main public holidays when virtually everything closes are:

1 January	New Year's Day
6 January	Epiphany
5 February	Constitution Day
21 March	Benito Juárez Day
March/April	Easter – Maundy Thursday, Good Friday and Easter Sunday
1 May	Labour Day
5 May	Battle of Puebla
15/16 September	Independence Day
12 October	National Day
20 November	Anniversary of the Revolution
12 December	Festival of the Virgin of Guadalupe
25 December	Christmas Day

In addition, every town or village will take at least one day off a year for a Fiesta – (see also section – **Fiestas**).

Details from the nearest tourist office *(turismo)*.

Lost Property

Report it to the local police headquarters if you can make yourself understood, or if it is something more serious, a lost passport, for instance, report it to your embassy or consulate.

Media

Press

The daily English-language newspaper, the *Mexico City News*, is available in Mexico City and larger towns and resorts. There are also free English-language news-spreads such as the *Daily Bulletin* which can be picked up in Mexico City or tourist centres – either in large hotels or from tourist offices. American, British and other foreign newspapers are available from large hotels and bookshops, such as *Sanborn's*, though a few days late.

Radio

Mexico City's *Radio XEVIP* (AM 1560) broadcasts news and programmes in English throughout the day. Stations in other cities have several hours of English-language programmes each day. In some parts of the country, American radio broadcasts can be picked up, while the *BBC World Service* is also received, the best reception on 11.75 MHz, in the evening.

Money Matters

Mexico's unit of currency is the **peso**, comprising 100 **centavos**. Since devaluation in 1993 new coins and notes marked **nuevo** (new) **peso** are in circulation. Coins range from 5c (centavos) to 50 pesos. Notes range from 10 to 500 pesos.

The new peso should be written N\$ and American dollars as US\$. Sometimes certain expensive shops and hotels do not make it clear which currency they are referring to.

Currency rates can fluctuate daily due to the **peso's** weakness against other strong currencies. Banks and exchange houses *(Casas de Cambio)* offer competitive rates. Avoid changing large amounts in hotels and always check rates as some hotel exchange fees are as high as 15 per cent.

Fiesta is the spirit of Mexico

Credit cards and travellers cheques in US dollars and US dollars themselves are widely accepted in the larger cities and resorts.

Many hotels, restaurants and some stores and markets accept US dollars (often at a worse rate); it is a good idea to carry a small calculator as well as some local currency. To avoid fraud it is wise to make sure 'NP' is clearly marked on credit card receipts. Horde small coins and notes to pay buses, taxis and porters and don't embarrass yourself by trying to change large notes in inexpensive venues.

Opening Times

It is almost impossible to generalise about opening times in Mexico – even when times are posted in museums, shops, etc, they are not strictly adhered to. The *siesta* is still widely in evidence, usually from 13.00 to 15.00hrs but for up to four hours along the hotter Gulf Coast and in the Yucatán. In the north and highland areas hours are more standard and there is sometimes no siesta.

Times below present a general picture:

Offices: 08.00–15.00hrs Monday to Friday.

Shops: *(Mexico City)* 09.00–20.00hrs Monday to Saturday *(Elsewhere)* 09.00–14.00hrs and 16.00–20.00hrs Monday to Friday.

Banks: 09.00–13.30hrs Monday to Friday. (Exchange houses – *Casas de Cambio* are open until later.)

Post Offices: 08.00–18.00hrs Monday to Friday (in large cities).

Museums/ Galleries: Generally 09.00–13.00hrs and 15.00–18.00hrs, but closed Sunday afternoons and all day Monday.

Archaeological Sites: Open all day.

Personal Safety

Despite alarmist reports about *banditos*, Mexico is a surprisingly safe place to travel. You should, however, not act in such a way as to draw attention to yourself and in any confrontation back off. Large cities and areas of political unrest demand extra attention. After dark use well-lit streets, and avoid lonely train stations, underpasses and public parks (see also **Crime**).

A bigger threat to personal safety is perhaps through a natural event – the threat of a future disastrous earthquake is forever there, especially in Mexico City!

Pharmacist

Look for a green cross and the word *farmacia*. Pharmacists can be very useful, most speak English and are able to diagnose and treat minor ailments. Many drugs are often available without the prescription necessary in Britain or the USA, but be warned, some drugs are on sale which have been banned elsewhere. The most common ailment of visitors to Mexico is diarrhoea, known as *turista* – most pharmacists are well used to this problem and the single word *diarrea* is often enough to be given the appropriate medicine.

In every town at least one *farmacia* remains open 24 hours, known as the *farmacia de la guardia* – hotel receptionists or tourist offices should be able to tell you which one.

Places of Worship

Mexico is a Catholic country (93 per cent) and, no matter how small a village is, there is bound to be a church there. The Catholic services are in Spanish, but it is possible to find services in English in Mexico City, Guadalajara, Cuernavaca, Acapulco and Monterrey. Until relatively recently women needed to cover their heads when entering churches; this is not always the case today. Your hotel, the local tourist office or your consulate will be able to supply you with addresses and times of services, and English services are listed in *The News* every Friday. The following is a selection of places of worship with English-language services.

Acapulco

Catholic:	Maranatha Church, Calle Juan Sebastian.
Episcopal:	Holy Cross Episcopal Church, behind Hotel Las Vegas.
Interdenomi-national:	Chapel of Peace, Las Brisas.
Jewish:	Shalom Restaurant, Posada del Sol.

Cuernavaca

Catholic:	Third Order Catholic Church on cathedral grounds.
Episcopal:	St Michael and All Angels Episcopal Church, Guerrero at Degollado.

Guadalajara

Baptist:	Gethsemane Baptist Church, Colomos 2148.

Catholic:	Our Lady of Guadalupe, Tepeyac; and Fr Juan de Zumamaga, Colonia Chapalita.
Episcopal:	St Mark's, Azteca and Chichimecas, in Colonia Lomas del Valle.

Mexico City

Baptist:	Capital City Baptist Church, Bondojito and Calle Sur 138.
Catholic:	St Patrick's, Bondojito 248; and Our Lady of Lourdes, Castillo de Chapultepec 70, Lomas de Chapultepec.
Episcopal:	Christ Church Episcopal, Calle Sierra Madre 210, Colonia las Lomas.
Jewish:	Beth Israel Community Centre, Virreyes 1140; Nidjei Israel Synagogue, Calle Acapulco 70; Mount Sinai Temple, Querétaro 110.

Monterrey

Episcopal:	Holy Family, Somberete and Teotihuacán.
Interdenomi-national:	Union Church of Monterrey, Oscar Castillon 200.

Police

The District Police Force maintains public order and safety and is in charge of traffic control. The police have certain duties relating specifically to visitors and their protection: to prevent private citizens from acting as unauthorized guides; to prevent the detention of foreign citizens or vehicles over small violations (though you should not take this as an excuse to violate the laws); to look out for merchants who raise their prices; and to give information and directions. If you park illegally, your licence plates may be taken away. If this happens, or if you commit a minor traffic violation, you may be able to rectify the situation by offering the policeman a 'fine'; these *mordidas* (little bites) are quite common and may be suggested by the officer.

A special 'Language Police Force' is planned in Mexico City for the benefit of English-speaking visitors.

Post Office

Mexican postal services (*correos*) can be very slow, though fairly dependable. Airmail to the USA takes around a week, and two weeks to Europe and other destinations. If mail is important take it to the post office rather than drop it in a post box. You can also buy stamps and post mail through your hotel desk. Do not hand in money for stamps along with your cards – they may not arrive. For essential and reliable fast service use Mexpost, which operates within post offices (or DHL, Federal Express).

Public Transport

Air

Travel within Mexico is expensive and some thirty main airports throughout the country are serviced by the two major domestic lines, *Mexicana* and *Aeroméxico*. Other domestic airlines also provide a service. In recent years, air fares to different towns and cities throughout Mexico have shown themselves to be governed by competition. A route where there is little competition and not much traffic is likely to be more expensive than a route where their is inter-airline competition because the traffic is busy. Shop around, sometimes you can save money by going via another city to reach your destination.

There is a departure tax of around US$9 on internal flights which is often built into the cost of the ticket.

Rail

Starting with main stations, Tijuana and Mexicali in the north, the networks service important central and coastal cities and venture as far south as Mérida in the east and Tapachula in the west. The comfort of rail travel in Mexico is to a great extent governed by cost. Second class (*segunda clase*) travel is cheap but the seats are poorly padded and the carriages inclined to be crowded and hot or cold according to the weather outside. The scene may be picturesque but uncomfortable. Regular first class (*primera general clase*) carriages are usually air conditioned, comfortable and less crowded. In first class, *Primera Reservada* (or *Especial*), you get a reserved seat (usually reclining), in an air-conditioned and roomy carriage. For sleepers you pay a supplement over the top first class rate. The least expensive are curtained off bunks (*camas*), in Pullman-style carriages.

It is advisable to book fares in advance and to double check on the class of service available. The official guide is not always correct. In smaller stations, tickets are not often sold until the train arrives in the station. If you board without a ticket, the collector will charge an extra 25 per cent on the fare. If tickets are sold out, try to buy direct from the porter for a few extra dollars.

Buses

The most common and efficient form of public transport. Seven hundred bus lines operate in Mexico itself, and despite the size of the country there is hardly a place that cannot be reached by bus. Fares are very cheap and there is a first (*primera*) and second (*segunda*) class service, and now on many routes a super executive class called *Ejectivo*. Few second class vehicles are new. They are eventually relegated to junkyards but that can take quite a long time, so they can be fairly uncomfortable. First class tickets assign seats and some second class new buses, which operate long haul routes, do the same. Generally speaking, second class services are far more

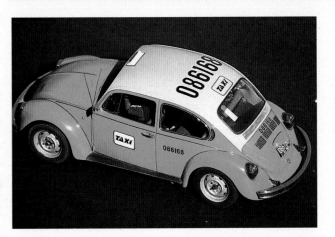

Mexico City's taxis are 'green' in both senses of the word!

crowded, less comfortable and noisier than first class. On your first class ticket is marked the number of the bus (*camión*), the hour of departure and the destination. Upon purchase, make sure you check that the details on your ticket are correct.

Luggage can be checked through to your final destination and you need to retain your check stub for collection.

Urban Services

In Mexico City there is an excellent and cheap metro system, with frequent trains and a flat fare. There is also a small tramway network and extensive bus and trolley-bus services. The latter has recently been modernised and operates a flat fare system.

(See also **Mexico City – Transport**).

Guadalajara has a state-run bus and underground trolley service, also extensive private buses.

Taxis

Only in Mexico City are you likely to find metered taxis. Every city has its own system. Establish your fare before booking your ride. Short town trips are not expensive but taxis to the airport are, so find out if your hotel has a pick-up coach service.

Colectivos – usually VW minibuses – have set routes that will take you to suburbs or large cities and out-of-town destinations. This type of shared taxi service is cheap, and their destinations are written on the outside.

Senior Citizen Travel

Benefits to senior citizens (over 60) similar to students are also available. Write to Instituto Nacional de Lasenectuo, Concepcion Beistegui 13, Col Deivaille 03100, Mexico DF (tel: (5) 536-24-88 and (5) 536-24-59).

DIRECTORY

Student Travel

There are considerable benefits connected with travelling and visiting places of interest, available to students with the right documentation, and those planning their holiday in advance and wishing to take advantage of these opportunities should write to CREA, Serapío Rendon 76, Colonía San Rafael, Mexico 06470 DF (tel: (5) 546-85-05 and (5) 591-01-44).

Telephones

Long-distance and international calls from Mexico are very expensive and it is advisable to place reversed charge calls (*por cobrar*) when calling home. This works out at half the price, or less, of direct-dial calls, though you can be charged whether you get through or not. Calls out of Mexico can be

Calling home is very expensive!

placed anywhere displaying the blue-and-white *Larga Distancia* sign. Most *Telefonos* offices also offer the service. Unless you wish to make a direct-dial call, the procedure is that you dial 09 for the English-speaking international operator who connects you and presents you with a bill afterwards (you can keep an eye on the cost which clicks up on a meter). You can also make calls from hotels but they always carry an add-on price, so check first.

Local calls in Mexico on the other hand are ridiculously cheap. To make long-distance calls within Mexico dial 92, plus the telephone code and number (station to station), or 92 plus the telephone code and number (person to person). For the national operator call 02; for information dial 04.

To call Mexico from abroad dial the international access code (00 from Britain), plus the code for Mexico (52), followed by the area code, then the number. Phoning in Mexico can be frustrating and you need time and patience. Public and private faxes are available.

Time

Mexico spans three time zones. Expressed in relation to Greenwich Mean Time (GMT) these are:

General Mexico Time (GMT minus 6)
– General, Coahuila, Durango, Nuevo Léon, and Tamaulipas.
Mountain Time (GMT minus 7)
– Nayarit, Sinaloa, Sonora, and Baja California Sur.
Pacific Time (GMT minus 8)
– Baja California Norte.

Daylight Saving
Comes into operation in some parts of Mexico during the summer, when clocks are put forward an hour. This affects the areas: Coahuila, Durango, Nuevo León, and Tamaulipas where local time becomes GMT minus 5, while time in Baja California Norte becomes GMT minus 7.

Tipping
Service charges are rarely added to hotel, restaurant or waiter-service bar bills, a tip should be given in these circumstances. Waiters expect 10–20 per cent of the bill if no service charge has been added. Porters get at least 2 new pesos per bag. Taxi drivers do not expect tips unless you have small change left over or you hire them for several hours. Ushers and washroom attendants receive small gratuities.

Toilets
Public toilets are known usually as *baños* (literally 'bathrooms') or as *excusados*, *sanitarios* or *servicios*. They are mostly unhygienic affairs, with a shortage of paper (though it may be sold outside). Most often you will see the signs *Damas* (Ladies) and *Caballeros* (Gentlemen), otherwise you will come across the potentially confusing *Señoras* (Women) and *Señores* (Men).

Tourist Offices
The *Secretaria de Turismo* (*SecTur*) has offices (*Turismo*) in Mexico City and throughout the country. Their main office is at:

Presidente Masaryk 172, 11587 Mexico City (tel: (5) 250-8555). There is a 24-hour tourist information 'hotline': (5) 250-1023.

In addition there are tourist offices run by state and municipal authorities and often you will find several rival operations in the same town. The local telephone directory gives the address and phone number of both federal and local tourist offices.

LANGUAGE

Pronunciation
Vowels All Spanish vowel sounds are pure. The final **e** is always pronounced.

Pronounce	a	as in (father)
	e	as in (bed)
	ai	as in (air)
	i	as in (machine)
	o	as in (low)
	u	as in (ruin)

Consonants
Similar to English consonants with some exceptions, ie:

Pronounce		
	n	as in (canyon)
	ll	as a 'y' (yoghurt)
	g	as 'h' except when followed by 'u'
	h	is silent
	qu	as 'k' (cane)

Words which end in a vowel, **n** or **s** are stressed on the last syllable but one, eg **ca**sa, **ga**fas, **ven**den. Words which end in a consonant other than **n** or **s** are stressed on the last syllable, eg ha**blar**, espa**nol**. A written accent mark will indicate

LANGUAGE

exceptions to this rule, eg café, autobús, estación.

Numbers

1	uno
2	dos
3	tres
4	cuatro
5	cinco
6	seis
7	siete
8	ocho
9	nueve
10	diez
11	once
12	doce
13	trece
14	catorce
15	quince
16	diez y seis
17	diez y siete
18	diez y ocho
19	diez y nueve
20	veinte
21	veinte y uno
22	veinte y dos
23	veinte y tres
24	veinte y cuatro
30	treinta
40	cuarenta
50	cincuenta
60	sesenta
70	setenta
80	ochenta
90	noventa
100	cien (or) ciento
1000	mil

Days of the Week

Monday	Lunes
Tuesday	Martes
Wednesday	Miércoles
Thursday	Jueves
Friday	Viernes
Saturday	Sábado
Sunday	Domingo

Months (meses)

January	Enero
February	Febrero
March	Marzo
April	Abril
May	Mayo
June	Junio
July	Julio
August	Agosto
September	Septiembre
October	Octubre
November	Noviembre
December	Diciembre

Basic Phrases

Good morning/good day Buenos días

Good afternoon Buenas tardes

Good evening/good night Buenas noches

Good-bye Adiós

Hello Hola

How are you? Cómo está usted?

Very well, thank you Muy bien, gracías

See you soon Hasta luego

Have a good journey Buen viaje!

Good luck/all the best Buena suerte!

Sorry/excuse me Perdone

That's all right Está bien

Everything all right? De nada?

Don't worry No se preocupe

It doesn't matter No importa

I beg your pardon? Qué/cómo dice?

Am I disturbing you? (Le) molesto?

I'm sorry to have troubled you Siento haberle molestado

Good/that's fine Bien/está muy bien

I don't feel well Me siento mal/no me siento mal

Where is the bathroom/WC? Donde está el baño?

I have a reservation. My name is ... Tengo una reservacion. Me llamo ...

INDEX/ACKNOWLEDGEMENTS

The Automobile Association would like to thank the following photographers and libraries for their assistance in the preparation of this book:

AA PHOTO LIBRARY Peter Wilson took all the photographs with the exception of the cover, 42, 49, 66, 89 and 123 which were taken by R Strange

MARY EVANS PICTURE LIBRARY 21 Spaniards destroy Aztec sculptures, 22 Cortés advances

NATURE PHOTOGRAPHERS LTD 91 Cardon cactus (P R Sterry), 92 Flycatcher, 93 Large forest butterfly (N P Williams), 94 Great blue heron (P R Sterry), 95 Green lizard, 97 Usumacinta Marshes (N P Williams), 99 Gray whale, 100 Los Islotes (P R Sterry)

SPECTRUM COLOUR LIBRARY 34 Museum of Anthropology

ZEFA PICTURE LIBRARY (UK) LTD 119 Fiesta

MEXICAN TOURIST BOARD 6/7 Island of Janitzio, 8 Baja California

Thanks to **Peter McGregor Eadie** for his revision work